THE END OF MAN

The End of Man

Jean-Paul Martinon

punctum books ✳ brooklyn, ny

First published in 2013 by
punctum books
Brooklyn, New York
http://punctumbooks.com

ISBN-13: 978-0615766782
ISBN-10: 0615766781

Library of Congress Cataloging Data is available from the Library of Congress.

Cover Image: detail from Jacques-Louis David, *Male Nude Known as Hector* (1778); oil on canvas, Musée Fabre, Montpellier, France.

Facing-page drawing by Heather Masciandaro.

Table of Contents

Acknowledgements

A project of this kind can only be accomplished with the help and encouragement of many friends and individuals. To some I owe a special thanks. I am particularly grateful to Nicole Wolf, Michael O'Rourke, Eileen A. Joy, Sam Nightingale, Lynn Turner and Kamillea Aghtan. My thanks also to my colleagues in the Department of Visual Cultures and especially Jorella Andrews for allowing the impossible: taking a three-month sabbatical in the middle of the academic year.

Many of the ideas in this book have been tried out on doctoral students and staff at Goldsmiths College, first as part of a seminar organised by INC Research Group in Continental Philosophy and later as part of the Visual Cultures PhD Programme. Thanks are due to all those who have listened, questioned, and challenged the ideas that follow. I am grateful to learn from an amazing community of artists, scholars and thinkers.

Nunhead, London, 2012

Introduction

At the time of bands such as The Cult and Jad Wio, friends would often find me in dark corners of cavernous nightclubs dressed in black leather with eyeliner carefully applied inside the eye and grey eye shadow on the lower eyelid in order to accentuate the deathly appearance. My hair would be shoulder length and ironed straight. Underneath my jacket, I would wear a vest made of gaping black fishnet material. Nine earrings would adorn my left ear and numerous leather and old-silver bracelets would grace my wrists. I remember feeling proud of my skeletal frame and ultra-thin arms. In appearance, I was a gender-bender, but in reality, my sexual life was simply undefined and unexplored.

At the time of bands such as Goldfrapp and La Rue Ketanou, friends would often find me in the brightly lit spaces of health-clubs dressed in shorts, sneakers, and t-shirt with only moisturizer on my face. My hair would be a number one crew cut. In my left hand, I would carry an energy drink. After my workout, which consisted of a split-routine entirely designed to achieve maximum upper-body muscle growth, I would gulp down with much effort a high-protein and carbohydrate shake.

I remember feeling proud of the tiny gains in muscle growth. For all intents and purposes, I was a dedicated gym buff with a clearly defined sexual identity.

At the time of bands such as Hanni El Khatib and DJs such as Sebastian Akchoté, friends would occasionally find me in the sanitized world of fertility clinics dressed in a non-descriptive way except for headphones as my sole distinctive feature. In my right hand, I would carry a sample pot, sheepishly dropping it in a lidded bucket labelled 'Man Samples Only,' ready for analysis. The experience of having to coldly force something out of one's body when this very body only understands this activity through the prism of selfish pleasure is a perplexing one. This added to the fact that what has always been casually discarded is now examined for its potential to outlive me makes for a disconcerting experience. Fertility clinics are places where no one feels pride, just bafflement at the ways human beings attempt to control and manipulate bodily functions.

The above three moments reflect three different types of anxiety about being *a* man.

The first one is obviously rebellious, a way of questioning the idea of masculinity (and its supposed attributes: power, strength, virility, for example) from the advantage of youth. Through its own idiosyncratic dramatization of the signifying gestures of dress codes, it shows that it is not only aware of, but also relishes the performative nature of gender.

The second one plays the opposite card: it conforms to a type of ideology promoted by contemporary society for which a man needs to look like Mark Walhberg in his Calvin Klein heyday, a kind of pathological exception turned into a prescriptive norm. The self-awareness is here pushed to the limits because it does not aim to acquire a real and forbidding fleshy armour that would be typical of a supposed 'heterosexual' identity, but on the contrary, to embody a self-conscious cliché of artificial maleness.[1]

---

[1] And thus obeying what Susan Faludi calls an 'ornamental culture': "In a culture of ornament, manhood is defined by appearance, by youth and attractiveness, by money and aggression, by posture and swagger,

The third one is obviously an anxiety about one's ability to outlive oneself. It conforms to an unquestioned and supposedly innate imperative: to sustain humanity's ability to reproduce itself. In this way, the anxiety here is not entirely personal, it is also that of a world that asks itself, perhaps for the first time in history, whether it is worth reproducing at all. And while everything in fertility clinics emphasizes artificiality (from 'procurement rooms' to 'gynaecological chairs'), human beings stubbornly cling on to the last scrap of a seemingly obvious dignity: the 'natural' imperative to obey a commandment that is older than history itself.

There is nothing unusual or exceptional about this shortened and incomplete three-step trajectory; on the contrary, it is a commonplace narrative about masculinity, manhood, and fatherhood at the turn of the millennium. However, it also raises the question of how *a* man is supposed to articulate himself in a world where the meaning of these terms have been so dramatically questioned so as to become practically meaningless. The following text does not aim to be an exhaustive or comprehensive answer to that question. On the contrary, it attempts, with the use of a specific philosophical vocabulary and language, to revisit famous key concepts in the construction of masculinity, not in order to re-write or debunk them once more, but in order to provide a *personal* take on them.

I don't have long to live—twenty years if I compile both family history and society's statistics. So if I take this real or imaginary deadline as an imperative to work out 'what happened?', then one of the questions that inevitably comes up is indeed this: how do I articulate my masculinity, manhood, and fatherhood? This does not imply that I will dwell in personal anecdotes or autobiographical details. The above trajectory suffices. In reverse, this does not also imply that I will attempt to draw from my experiences either a generic perspective that would be applicable to all or an overarching theory of masculinity, maleness, and/or fatherhood. The aim is

---

and 'props,' by the curled lip and flexed biceps...": Susan Faludi, *Stiffed: The Betrayal of the American Man* (New York: Harper Perennial, 2000), 38.

simply to put forward a personal perspective on the *intractable* condition of being *one* man amongst many today.

The intractability of this 'condition' is really what is at stake here. The aim is not to just talk about 'me' or about what counts 'above all,' 'men,' as if these could be understood as autonomous and rational animals with free wills, the apex of existence. The following takes for granted that men are imperfect, disunited, and always prey to 'becoming' some'thing' else and as such are not singular entities that can be analysed as such.[2] The issue is on the contrary to emphasize this liminal 'condition' that is both produced *and* inscribed and prevents 'me' from ever ignoring or getting rid of this extra Y that appears to cause all the anxieties and insecurities mentioned above. If one takes in consideration this intractability, then, as the following text will attempt to show, I am; man is; or men are here neither first nor foremost. This liminal 'condition' or end is.

* * *

But what end? The end in question in this book does not refer to the completion of an act ('this is the end of the line for me'), the conclusion of a jury ('this really is a man'), a finished project ('nothing could be said after this'), or a subjective and arbitrary divination of the future, the result of a revelation without evidences, tributary of faith ('men, frankly, are doomed'). If this were the case, then the mention of the word 'end' would simply refer not only to a false interiority ('me' or 'us' as a clearly identified sum of past events), a false exteriority ('he' or 'them': all the fellows next door), or a new beginning (a post- or

---

[2] There is no space here to explore this topic. Suffice to say that this book obviously adheres to the idea that man or menfolk in general are not just self-contained humans, but a zoo of posthumanity, in the sense developed, for example, by Judith Halberstam and Ira Livingston, "Introduction: Posthuman Bodies," in *Posthuman Bodies*, ed. Judith Halberstam and Ira Livingston (Bloomington: Indiana University Press, 1995), 1–20 and Cary Wolfe, ed., *What Is Posthumanism?* (Minneapolis: University of Minnesota Press, 2009).

super-man). Patriarchy, masculinity, or men in general are not about to be wiped out; as far as I know I am not dead yet; and Aurobindo or Nietzsche's predictions about overmen[3] have not yet come into being.

The end in the title of this book is therefore not conceived— if this is really possible—as a *figured* end that would delimit or organize anthropologically *or* metaphysically a first person ('I'), a third ('he') or even a first person plural ('we, men'). In other words, the end in question here is not a representable line that would either picture or circumscribe 'me' or 'us, men' as if a clearly identifiable individual or group within humankind or as part of a generic set of abstract concepts. In order to avoid such a figured end (and therefore the inevitable accompanying assumptions about what lies beyond 'it': women or God, for example), it is necessary to think the end differently. But how?

One way, I think, an 'end' can be understood 'differently' is to remain *both* at a metaphysical *and* anthropological level. As is well known, the problem is indeed that it is simply impossible today to think of an anthropology without entrenching it in metaphysics.[4] If I talk about 'me' as an anthropological topic, for example, I can only embed this topic within a metaphysical

---

[3] See Sri Aurobindo, *The Life Divine* [1914-19] (Pondicherry: Sri Aurobindo Ashram Press, 1990) and Friedrich Nietzsche, *Thus Spoke Zarathustra*, trans. R.J. Hollingdale (London: Penguin, 1985).

[4] The most acute description of this problem can be found in a footnote of Derrida's famous text, "The Ends of Man." I give here an abbreviated version for lack of space: "A) *On the one hand*, it is precisely when Kant wants to conceive of something as the end, the pure end, the end in itself, that he must criticize anthropologism, in the *Metaphysics of Morals*.... In this manner, all morals which need anthropology for their application to men must be completely developed first, as pure philosophy, i.e. metaphysics, independently of anthropology... B) But *on the other hand*, ... man is the only example, the only case of a reasonable being that can ever be cited at that very point at which the universal concept of reasonable being can justifiably be distinguished from the concept of human being. It is at the point of this fact that anthropology recovers all of its authority which had been contested": Jacques Derrida, *Margins of Philosophy*, trans. A. Bass (Chicago: University of Chicago, 1982), 121–2.

framework—about the limits of this 'me,' for example. Inversely, it is not possible to think a metaphysical issue without entrenching it within an anthropological context. If I take 'man' as a metaphysical topic, for example, I can only assume that there is a world-wide abstract understanding of this word. The problem is such that it simply cannot be overcome. Metaphysics and anthropology cannot be understood independently of each other. But how is one then to understand, what one should really call a meta-anthropology? What other familiar name does it have?

Perhaps it is simply what is called bio-graphy. The biographical is here understood not in the common sense of 'an account of my life,' but in the sense of a formal organisation that would insinuate itself *between* metaphysics and anthropology. In order to understand this, it is necessary to abandon the idea that metaphysics and anthropology are *simply* institutional disciplines and to take up the parallel idea that they are *also* practices. This can be said very simply: as I live, I write (literally or metaphorically) my own bio-graphy.[5] In doing so, I am forced to delimit what I write not only in relation to others (thus defining myself in an anthropological context), but also in relation to what lies beyond this relation (thus defining myself in a metaphysical context). The bio-graphical is therefore a formal organization in as much as it is an attempt to trace the lived distinction between metaphysics and anthropology. In other words, the bio-graphical is what marks—*graphein*, to write—the dangerous delineation or passage between a spatially and temporally situated 'bio/me' and its ex-teriority or ex-cess.

---

[5] This does not imply treating myself as if another, but, following Derrida, as a type of writing that traces the experience of the impossible, an attempt to speak about what cannot be said, perceived, or be made present. The bio-graphical is therefore in this context what Derrida calls the "hetero-thanato-graphical": writing one's life as a matter of life-death. On this theme, see Jacques Derrida, *The Post Card: From Socrates to Freud and Beyond*, trans. A. Bass (Chicago: Chicago University Press, 1987), 273 and 291 and passim.

The end in the title of this book therefore refers to no limit, extremity, or finale *strictly speaking*, but to a formal organisation that in itself has no meaning, not because it is non-sense or absurd, but because it can only really prevaricate as that which separates and unites metaphysics and anthropology, and in the process, writes both of them at once. The end is therefore paradoxically both an aporia (a non-passage) and a poros (a passage) that structures both metaphysics and anthropology, not as institutional disciplines, but as everyday practices (articulating or writing not only *this* recognizable man, but also what has *as yet* no name for it). A bio-graphy is thus what writes itself as man as I, he, or we break(s) open the future.

The 'end' is in the singular because the aim is to emphasize this curious a-poretic aspect, this singular intractability. Since it is not possible to envisage all of the attributes of one man in one single coherent discourse or theory, then the question is really to uncover this aporia/poros that, for reasons that are both mine *and* not mine, reveals *this* man as suddenly appearing/disappearing at once. In this way, *The End of Man* effectively refers to a passage, not the clichéd thrusting passage into the other, but the im-proper passing into the unknown space and time of the other; a space and time that can never be understood as 'belonging' to what on all accounts can be 'seen' as *this* man. Against duration and multiplicity, *The End of Man* will then be this: *this* man is simply an end that bio-graphically marks the im-proper passing onto the other.

As one might expect when it comes to a-poretic situations, the issue is not so much the passage onto the other as if this 'other' can be understood as either 'another' self-contained bio-anthropological entity (a woman, for example) or a symbolic metaphysical radicality (God, for example), but to a wide range of subjects and objects, all of which have the unique characteristic of forming and inhabiting different (bio-graphical) spaces and times. The 'other' will therefore be here undetermined, not out of ignorance, neglect, lack of manners, or out of an andro-homo-phallo-centric need to occult women or God, but because to do otherwise would be to already project and therefore appropriate this 'other' as the same as 'me,' and therefore—if I can make such a generalisation—the same as 'us, men.' In other words, the focus of this book is this liminal formal organization or passing that gives onto, not a supposed 'opposite' of man, but an 'other' who or that cannot be defined because he, she, it, or they is/are always already to-come.

* * *

The structure of the following text is accidental. It simply follows the path of reading and thinking for this specific research project. Although a thread runs through the book, its chapters can be read independently of each other. The bibliography attached at the end of this short book is not intended to be exhaustive of the topic. It is only given as an indication of the sources that were used to make up the following arguments and as an indication of potential further reading. The hope behind such a methodology is two-fold: to avoid at all cost the assumption of (phallic) coherence and mastery ('I know what I am talking about') and to avoid playing the hidden game of buggery that scholarly work tirelessly entails ('I'm right, he or she is wrong'). This two-fold hope is not only intended to pay homage to the many human bodies, subjects, and voices that produce and consume texts and who do not easily fall for the usual blinkered and dogmatic views that society (and the academy) imposes on all of us, but also to ensure that the following book remains always on the verge of losing its metaphysical and anthropological footing.[6]

Having written this, I ought, nonetheless, to finish by clarifying a little the specific choice of scholarship that was used to write this book, especially with regards to the issue of time

---

[6] As such, this text will strive as much as possible to *not* resemble a body. As Jean-Luc Nancy remarks: "Plato wants discourse to have the well-constituted body of a big animal, with a head, stomach, and tail. So all of us, we, good Platonists of old standing, know and don't know what a discourse lacking a head and tail would be… We know it's nonsense, but we don't know what to make of this 'non-sense,' we don't see past the tip of sense. We always assent to sense: beyond sense, we lose

as it directly informs and structures the unusual liminality envisaged in *The End of Man*. The following text attempts to stay as close as possible to a particular philosophical tradition that emphasizes the inescapable distinction between homogeneous and heterogeneous times, a distinction originally put forward by both Martin Heidegger and Emmanuel Levinas and subsequently articulated by a number of authors in continental philosophy.[7] There is unfortunately no space to unpack this particular distinction in the narrow context of this introduction. However, for the sake of clarity, here is perhaps what can be said in the most telegraphic style imaginable:

Homogeneous time refers to any kind of linear temporality. It is a type of time that necessarily confuses time with history, and therefore with durations or narratives that are seen to perdure over a period of time. In what concerns us here, the most common example of homogeneous time is 'straight' time, i.e. the set of chrono-normative frames that regulate 'heterosexual' life. For example: growing up, marriage, work, reproduction and death. Each of these frames takes time and therefore can be articulated as a series of homogeneous times (linear, reproductive, cyclical, etc.). Now, this is not exclusive to 'heterosexuals.' Homogeneous time also refers to 'queer' time, i.e. to this other set of chrono-normative frames that regulate 'queer' life, for example: the transient, the fleeting, the contingent, i.e. anything that is unscripted by the conventions of family, inheritance, and child rearing. However transient, instant and nocturnal, each of these frames nonetheless takes time and therefore can also be articulated as a series of

---

our footing": Jean-Luc Nancy, *Corpus*, trans. R. A. Rand (New York: Fordham University Press, 2008), 13.

[7] For such distinction, see: Martin Heidegger, *The Concept of Time*, trans. W. McNeill (London: Blackwell, 1992) and Emmanuel Levinas, *Time and the Other*, trans. R. A. Cohen (Pittsburgh: Duquesne University Press, 1987). Since it is not possible to account here for the numerous books that further articulate such a divide, I can only point therefore in the direction of the bibliography included in a previous book: Jean-Paul Martinon, *On Futurity: Malabou, Nancy, and Derrida* (London: Palgrave, 2007).

homogeneous times, even if they are perceived as disjunctive ('I *live* a non-reproductive life'), intransitive ('I *live* without a care for tomorrow'), interruptive ('I *live* in rebellion against continuity and progress'), etc.[8] In any given context, homogeneous time is what allows us to understand ourselves as Foucauldian bio-political constructs and this whether we are 'heterosexual,' 'homosexual' or 'queer.'[9]

By contrast, heterogeneous time refers to the radical questioning of such linear or homogeneous time. This is a

---

[8] Incorporating 'queer' time within the context of homogeneous times implies making a necessary departure from the conventional assumption that 'queers' inhabit alternate temporalities. They don't. We don't. However long or short, 'queer' times still respect linear, teleological, and even chronological narratives. These include the historical temporalities, life schedules, and alternative economic practices deployed, for example, by Judith Halberstam in *In a Queer Time and Place*. However disruptive, Halberstam's temporalities still obey the paradigmatic aspects of homogeneous time. The same can be said of other formulations of 'queer' temporalities, like for example, those exposed by Eve Kosofsky Sedgwick in, amongst others, *Tendencies*. However they are formulated, 'queer' time resembles 'straight' time precisely because their very utterance can do nothing else but to obey the rules of linear, teleological and chronological development not only in order to make sense, but also and above all to be narrated as such. There would be no 'queer' time and above all no performative acts of experimental self-perception and filiation if there were no 'moments' of recollection, that is, efforts to create a *recognizable* time frame with a 'before' and an 'after.' On this topic, see: Judith Halberstam, *In a Queer Time and Place: Transgender Bodies, Subcultural Lives* (New York: New York University Press, 2005); Eve Kosofsky Sedgwick, *Tendencies* (London: Routledge, 1994). See also the following commentaries: Stephen M. Barber and David L. Clark, "Queer Moments: The Performative Temporalities of Eve Kosofsky Sedgwick," in *Regarding Sedgwick: Essays on Queer Culture and Critical Theory*, ed. Stephen M. Barber and David L. Clark (London: Routledge, 2002), 1–53 and Elizabeth Freeman, *Time Binds: Queer Temporalities, Queer Histories* (Durham: Duke University Press, 2010).

[9] These terms are placed here and in the rest of the book in inverted commas in order to highlight the fact that they are invented abstractions. For a further explanation on this, see chapter 5, "End(s) Meet."

really difficult thought because it is rebellious to any form of articulation. To put it as 'simply' as possible, heterogeneous time refers to a type of questioning[10] that is so radical and so extreme that it cannot even take the shape of a question, let alone the shape of an empirical fact and/or metaphorical idea. The heterogeneity of this particular time is so diverse and incommensurable that it is impossible to totalize or homogenize. It is what is strictly allergic to language and as such knows no measure, no language or translation. This, however, does not mean that it is otherworldly or divine and as such exists elsewhere as the radical or negative opposite of homogeneous time. Heterogeneous time *shoots through* homogeneous time every second of time.[11] It is that which disturbs all becomings, durations, and narratives, even those that are supposedly 'anachronous' or 'asynchronous.'[12] Heterogeneous

---

[10] A questioning that leads Heidegger to stop short at his famous final question: "Who is time? More closely: are we ourselves time? Or closer still: am I my time?": Heidegger, *The Concept of Time*, 22.

[11] There is no space here to explore the subtle difference between heterogeneous time and messianic time, but the use of Benjamin's famous expression ('shot through') is obviously intended to reference a similar radicality, one that affords no homogeneity, narrative, projection or prediction. See Walter Benjamin, "Theses in the Philosophy of History," in *Illuminations*, ed. Hannah Arendt, trans. Harry Zorn (London: Pimlico, 1973), 245–6.

[12] Once again, the only way 'anachronic' or 'asynchronic' identities can indeed make sense would be if a teleological and therefore synchronic duration allowed them to be heard. As such, they would necessarily always need to fall within the context of linear (i.e. homogeneous) temporalities (however *logically* interruptive or preposterous these are). This does not re-inscribe heteronormativity as the only mode of fashioning or understanding identities or histories. This only highlights the impossibility of escaping the teleological structure of words, phrases, and discourses. For an example of this kind of 'anachronic' or 'asynchronic' (but nonetheless synchronic) identity, see the remarkable work of Carolyn Dinshaw, especially in "Temporalities," in *Middle English*, ed. Paul Strohm (Oxford: Oxford University Press, 2007), 107–23. For excellent accounts of the problems historians face when addressing sexual taxonomies in general, see Madhavi Menon, "Spurning Teleology in Venus and Adonis," in *GLQ: A Journal of*

time is effectively what makes me speechless, in awe, or simply recoil in horror at the stupidity of what has just happened.

Taking this distinction as seriously as is *humanly* possible, the following book can therefore only make *occasional* references to the vast expanse of often conflicting and contradictory linear temporalities that usually criss-cross or assemble a life and this one in particular (affects, belongings, becomings, histories, etc.). The scarcity of these references is not intended to dismiss their importance or their (temporary) political potential. The aim is simply to avoid not only quick narratives about one particular sex or gender, but also generalizations about who 'I' am or 'what men are like.' The aim is therefore to explore how time and a specific gender articulate themselves and to examine in some detail our understanding of this gender's seductive, bizarre, awesome, frightening and pathetic occurrences.

As such, this text situates itself on the margins of the majority of texts written in the field of sexual and gender studies and more specifically, masculinity studies. This does not mean that this book is written in order to be deliberately obscurantist. To be on the margins is not to choose a marginal discourse, but to faithfully remain 'queer' about all these discourses, that is, to remain at odds with what is already established as the norm (queer theory included).[13] The reason for such marginality, oddness, or queerness is simply that the radicality of heterogeneous time (as briefly defined above and as referred to later in this book and elsewhere as the law of

---

Lesbian and Gay Studies 11, no. 4 (2005): 491–519 and Glenn Burger and Steven F. Kruger, "Introduction," in *Queering the Middle Ages*, ed. Glenn Burger and Steven F. Kruger (Minneapolis: University of Minnesota Press, 2001), xi–xxii.

[13] In saying this, I remain simply faithful to David Halperin's understanding of the word 'queer': "Queer is by definition *whatever* is at odds with the normal, the legitimate, the dominant": David Halperin, *Saint Foucault: Towards a Gay Hagiography* (Oxford: Oxford University Press, 1995), 62. See also, Jonathan Kemp's commentary on this definition in Jonathan Kemp, "Queer Past, Queer Present, Queer Future," *Graduate Journal of Social Science* 6, Special Issue 1 (2009): 12.

absolute heterogeneity) can never be, as this text will strive to demonstrate, either casually forgotten, weakened, or simply glossed over.[14] The marginality, or perhaps more precisely, the rogueishness[15] of *The End of Man* is therefore due to the impossibility of evading this radical questioning, the possibilities offered by an absolute interruption.

Finally, the following book is written at the intersection of three bodies of work: the works of Emmanuel Levinas, Jacques Derrida, and Jean-Luc Nancy. 'At the intersection' *only* because, as stated above, there will be here no commentaries on their work. *The End of Man* attempts instead to think further their remarkable arguments about masculinity, sexuality, and gender. For example, it takes on board Levinas's notion of paternity, but leaves aside its patriarchal connotations. At another level, it develops Derrida's idea of a choreography of sexual differences, but without leaving it stranded in a correlationist differential.[16] Finally, it adheres to Nancy's

---

[14] Just to be clear, the following text therefore places itself neither with nor against what has been called the temporal turn in Queer Theory, but perhaps slightly off-kilter, if this is at all possible. The reason for such oddness or queerness is simply to emphasize the impossibility of pitching a 'queer' or 'homo'-normative time against a 'straight' or 'hetero'-normative time. Whatever we do with our genitals or bodies changes nothing to the fact that the future remains, however we strive to predict it, always already radically unknown. For the scholarship marking this temporal turn, see the path-breaking special issue dedicated to 'queer' temporalities edited by Elizabeth Freeman in: *GLQ: A Journal of Lesbian and Gay Studies* 13, nos. 2–3 (2007), doi: 10.1215/10642684-2006-029, and the excellent, E.L. McCallum and Mikko Tuhkanen, eds., *Queer Times, Queer Becomings* (Albany: State University of New York Press, 2011). See also Michael O'Rourke's clear analyses on the same topic in "The Afterlives of Queer Theory," *continent.* 1.2 (2011): 102–16.

[15] For this expression, see Michael O'Rourke's roguish, but nonetheless prudent and scholarly essay: "The Roguish Future of Queer Theory," *SQS: Journal of Queer Studies in Finland* 2 (2006): 22–47.

[16] There is no space or need here to mount a critique of Derrida's work within the framework of speculative realism. Suffice to say that it is impossible today to not acknowledge the fact that Derrida never really

understanding of the body as an ex-scription[17] of sense, but without turning it into an ecstatic, but strangely infertile reformulation of Christian incarnation. The aim of such an 'intersectional' work is simply to venture forth into the unknown, just when I can no longer recognize their writing or mine.

---

manages to give shape to his idea that sexual difference stands for a relentless choreography imposed by différance. How do we dance otherwise? How do we sustain the challenge against the locus, the certain, the established: male, female? Derrida remains silent. This does not mean that we should damn him as enthusiastic speculative realists often do. This simply means that it is now time to expose the shape of this dance, the many ways of playing the game. For a good analysis of Derrida and sexual difference, see Anne-Emmanuelle Berger, "Sexing Différance," in *Differences: A Journal of Feminist Cultural Studies* 16, no. 3 (2005): 52–67.

[17] "To write, and to read, is to be expected, to expose oneself, to this not-having (to [Bataille's] non-knowledge) and thus to 'exscription.' The exscribed is exscribed from the very first word, not as an 'inexpressible' or as an 'un-inscribable' but, on the contrary, as writing's opening, within itself, *to* itself, to its own inscription as the infinite discharging of meaning—in all the senses in which we must understand the expression": Jean-Luc Nancy, "Exscription," in *The Birth to Presence*, trans. K. Lydon (Stanford: Stanford University Press, 1993), 338.

1. The Neuter

It is neuter. This does not mean that it has been neutered. It started neuter. It plays and works neuter and the same can be said when it is eating, drinking, or relieving itself. There is no moment that can be pinpointed as being 'not-neuter.' Even when it sleeps, it remains neuter. And when it wakes up, like it does now on a lazy summer afternoon, it is still neuter, even with its hard-on. It never ceases to be neuter, even when it is weak or about to die. How is one to understand this odd neuter?

The contradictions of the above paragraph need not be emphasized: an erection is not neuter; it is an enlarged and rigid biological protuberance that clearly indicates that a man is in question here. However, over and beyond (or under and beneath) this bio-anthropological determination, is there not (also) something utterly neuter about 'it'?

Although the neuter in question here refers somewhat to the body, it does not stand for 'the body' *as such*. The neuter is not a generic physical structure comprehensible by all or a symbolic substitute for mankind in general. If this were the case, then the two (the body and the neuter) would be confused to the point of being interchangeable. The neuter has something to do with the body, but it is not '*the* body.'

And it is not 'the soul,' 'the spirit' or 'a monad' either. If this were the case, then the neuter would be a transcendental referent (representing a reductive entity or a superior consciousness, for example) that, in order to exist would somehow need to be put in relation with 'the body.' The neuter evades both these false dichotomies and these unnecessary reductions or elevations.

Just so that there is no confusion; the neuter in question here is also not Dasein. As is well known, Heidegger understands Dasein qua Dasein as sexually neutral.[17] He even talks of an originary and powerful asexual neutrality (*Neutralität*). In saying this, Heidegger's aim is to think Dasein as a primordial structure that sustains the binary of sexes. Dasein is therefore sexually *neutral* because as Dasein it does not carry with it the mark of this opposition (or alternative) between the two sexes.

As will become clear, the neuter in the following text departs from this interpretation for a simple reason: it insists on using the word neuter and not neutral. The neuter specifically relates to sex and gender, while the neutral can be understood as unrelated to these terms. This simple reason allows for a re-thinking of sex and gender that is not necessarily related to what could lie out-, in-, or along-side of it: Dasein qua Dasein. Having said this, the following text still retains Heidegger's insight that, like the neutral, the neuter is (also) what disperses the body. The question—and this is what will need to be addressed—is whether it can do this without relating to Dasein also dispersing itself positively in its facticity.

Finally, the neuter in question here is not a desire. Roland Barthes famously made this move from the neuter as a state to the desire for the neuter in order to a) avoid essentializing it, b) suspend (*épochè*) all forms of orders and, c) by way of

---

[17] See Martin Heidegger, *Being and Time,* trans. J. Macquarrie and E. Robinson (New York: Harper Collins, 1962), §10.

deepening, refuse all forms of opposition (including gender).[18] This move will not be repeated here because what concerns us above all is to expose not only the contradictory nature of the neuter (it includes oppositions and negotiates orders), but also, in a more Barthean move, its complexity, the fact that it cannot be totalized.

With these side-glances towards Heidegger and Barthes in mind, the neuter will therefore be presented most simply as a spatial and temporal quasi-bodily movement that cannot be distinguished from the advent of space and time.[19]

Please note: once again, there will be no assumption here that the addressee of this text will identify with this neuter, saying, for example 'Oh, yes, I identify myself in this neuter' or 'This neuter feels just like me.' The reason being that the word 'neuter' names in fact something that *can* be recognized, but *cannot* be made generic. As such, the neuter can only offer itself as a word that always misses on the opportunity of being pinned down and therefore shared as a generic characteristic common to all.

The neuter will therefore be here idiosyncratic to the one who addresses it with all its flaws and qualities. As such, this neuter will probably amuse, occasionally annoy, or even perhaps, in some acute moments, infuriate. Unfortunately, nothing can be done to stop this. This neuter simply 'is'—without 'being' exactly. The addressee—whoever he or she

---

[18] See Roland Barthes, *The Neutral: Lecture Course at the Collège de France (1977-1978)*, trans. R. E. Krauss and D. Hollier (New York: Columbia University Press, 2005), especially, 188–95.

[19] Although Jean-Luc Nancy does not specifically address the neuter, his understanding of the body and how it relates to the advent of space and time are crucial here. As he says, for example: "Space and time are the two names for birth; this double name is necessary so that there is a coming, weighing, or lifting of event, which is neither a point nor a present (neither space nor time), but presentation (imperfection). In this way, space is no longer spread and riddled with landmarks; time is no longer irreversible and a line of successions, but one by the other open, not just opened, but opening: the opening of a place, the taking-place of this place": Jean-Luc Nancy, *La Naissance des seins* (Valence: École régionale des beaux-arts, 1996), 17, my translation.

is—can either put up with it or just leave it and move over to the next section.

Unfortunately, those who can bravely ignore flaws and qualities and are able to stick with this neuter will face a rather abstract exposure. Although occasional glimpses towards more figurative horizons will be made in the aim of relieving the dryness of the abstraction, entertainment, in this first chapter, cannot be guaranteed. Unfortunately, this neuter suffers from being unable to sit long enough for it to be figured or represented and therefore pinned down for judgement... but I let you judge.

REFERENCE

Going against its well-known etymological origin, this neuter will not be understood here as what is 'neither this nor that,' 'neither one nor the other.' To refer to this etymological origin assumes the following question: if it is 'neither this nor that,' then 'what is it'? The reference therefore assumes the possibility of a third option: a flaw or a relief from the proposed alternative: this or that. But, as will be shown, this neuter is not a third option or an impersonal 'one' and it cannot be understood as the question that leads to the third.

Foreign to this familiar etymology, this neuter therefore has to be accepted as an event, whether it is this or that *and even* if it is neither this nor that. The problem with an event is that it can never be totalised; it cannot be part of a calculus or a reasoning system. The neuter simply escapes all forms of totalisation. Inversely, this neuter cannot be hollowed out of all contents; it cannot be emptied or made into a vacuum. The neuter in question here is effectively that which always lends itself to be totalised or hollowed out, but never manages to accomplish either of these states. This is the first alienating aspect of this neuter, the hallmark of any event (that of being this 'man,' for example).

However much it is alienating and evasive, one thing is certain: Contrary to popular opinion, this neuter is not an inanimate thing and it is not something inert or passive. The neuter in question here is both, curiously, animate and inanimate, active and passive, inert and dynamic. It strangely has all these characteristics. The most annoying aspect of this state of affairs is that neither its animate nor its inanimate aspects, for example, can be identified independently from the other. They 'cohabit' making up this neuter as it manifests itself.

IT, ALWAYS

As such, this neuter is not very seductive. There is no fantasy of neutrality, impartiality, or unbiased positioning hiding here under the non-nomination 'neuter.' As celebrities tirelessly remind us, only what marks itself as different or exceptional (within or outside of the neither/nor scheme) manages to seduce. The neuter in question here is far too complex to be truly seductive. It attracts and repels at the same time even when it gently awakes as it does right now.

This lack of seductiveness makes it perversely equivocal. This equivocality prevents anyone from identifying it as *a subject* with any certainty. In other words, it never comes across as a speaking person or a thinking and feeling entity. This neuter is effectively always already open to interpretation, questioning, probing, never finished or completed. This equivocal 'nature' never allows it to be anchored as something determinable that would be a part or a structure of subjectivity, for example—even if this subjectivity is understood as always performing or simply to-come.

Paradoxically, this lack of seductiveness also prevents it from being treated as *an object*, let alone a 'proper' object of study. In other words, it simply can never be objectified as such. Although it is the topic of this first chapter, the convoluted ways of describing it—avoiding at all cost 'neither-nor' sentences and therefore third options—shows that it can never be understood as a solid mass or an ethereal matter that can be scrutinised by either objective sciences or subjective narration.

But, and however contradictory this sounds, it nonetheless allows itself to be recognizable *both* as some 'one' who deserves attention (someone who deserves a kiss or a slap in the face, for example) and as a mere 'thing' that deserves to be indexed, identified, dissected, analysed, and then (inevitably) discarded. While the ontic sciences (physics when it comes to the neuter as object or psychoanalysis when it comes to the neuter as subject, for example) congratulate themselves in their attempts to master it, the question always remains: which of the two (some 'one' or a mere 'thing') will you choose? In other words, what is it: an object or a subject?

Unfortunately, *this* neuter cannot help you decide. It will remain always already both equivocally subject *and* object. As such, this neuter can therefore never be a pure 'I' or 'you' and it can never be a 'He' or a 'She' either. It remains irritatingly 'it,' not quite substantive, not quite being, maybe the very work of being an 'I' or a 'you,' a 'she' or a 'he.' 'Maybe' only, for it is impossible to assume a clear and distinctive relation between this neuter and either of these pronouns.

A-BODY

All this might lead one to think that the neuter is a non-body, a Stoic or Deleuzian incorporeal,[20] or some impersonal lack of distinction that unites or characterizes us all under the sun, for example. This couldn't be further from this neuter. This neuter is corporeal; it is a body with organs, hairy, bulky, smelly. It has bodily functions. It pisses and it cries. In doing so, it soils and leaves marks of difference.

And yet, this neuter cannot be reduced to a body strictly speaking. The reason being that this neuter never lets itself be recognized as an entity that can be identified: a body in need of relief or medication, for example. This neuter sweats, but it is never 'that which sweats': a 'sweator,' for example. The same goes for ejaculations, defecations, tears, and bad breaths. No

---

[20] See Gilles Deleuze, *The Logic of Sense*, trans. M. Lester (London: Continuum, 2003), 8–9.

particular bodily function can identify it because it comes *with* the process of identification, *with* the recognition that it is an '*I* who sweats,' a '*he* who suffers from hyperhidrosis,' a '*we* who ejaculate, defecate, or stink.' This neuter is therefore clearly not quite a body as such.

In this way, this neuter—i.e. this odd body/non body—can only make sense when it becomes manifest, that is, when it encounters other bodies, other things, other objects—someone's anus or the porcelain of a urinal, for example. Without these other bodies, without these other things, there would be no neuter, for they are what allows it to become manifest, not as if an alter-ego or hostage-taker,[21] not as if a receptacle or an undetermined background, but as the condition that allows friction between things and beings in general.

This does not mean that there is 'a friction' called 'the neuter' that would exist between bodies or non-bodies, not even when there is evidence: a rash or a slash, for example. The neuter becomes manifest but never turns into a manifestation in its own right. It is 'the other'—as un/defined in the Introduction—that or who presupposes and determines—but not exclusively—this neuter that knows no proper bodily or ethereal referent.

---

[21] This references Levinas's argument that the other holds me 'hostage.' To say the opposite is not a way of contradicting or going against Levinas, it is simply an attempt to think the situation in which the other indeed holds us 'hostage' and yet paradoxically we are (also) the hostage-takers, a 'condition' of friction that puts less emphasis on the necessarily overwhelming interference of the radically other 'in me.' I develop this argument in *After 'Rwanda'* (Amsterdam: Rodopi, 2013). Here is an example of how Levinas describes the situation of always already being a hostage of the other: "We are always someone else's hostage, but not so that we can go and complain about it": Emmanuel Levinas and Michaël de Saint Cheron, *Conversations with Emmanuel Levinas, 1983-1994* (Pittsburgh: Duquesne University Press, 2010), 37.

THE COMPLEX

This odd animate/inanimate, body/non-body status does not mean that it is unreal. The neuter looses no grip on (or a sense of) reality. In the same way that it only becomes manifest when encountering 'the other,' it is also affected by others (bodies or things) and this friction of affects gives it its reality. The problem is that, unfortunately, the reality in question here can never be totalised. Indefinite, the neuter can terrify as it relaxes; it can calm as it becomes exasperated: contradictory states that can take place simultaneously.

In doing so, the neuter therefore exposes both reality's distinctiveness (its recognizable sharp and urgent features, for example), but also its strangeness (what makes it remain always incomprehensible, for example). In other words, the neuter fuses with reality without disappearing altogether and in the process reveals reality as well as its (own) contradictions.

In this way and to follow Roland Barthes' well-known line of thought, this neuter is "the complex;"[22] it consists of many different parts that annoyingly can never be made one because they fuse with other realities. As such, the neuter can never be a neat juxtaposition of body and soul or a complex network of flesh, blood, and organs—not even when it slowly turns into a corpse. It just consists of many different parts, each of which come and go logically, but also, paradoxically, without any proper logic or rationale.

As such, the neuter is what is unbearable to doxa, withstands received opinion, and annoys the middle classes and their numbing (virtual) chitchat. But this does not mean that it is a vague or a fuzzy concept, like 'the androgyne' or 'consciousness,' for example. Real bio-graphical organizations (such as *this* neuter lying here in the sun) do not exclude concreteness. The neuter is 'here' embodying a sleeping man, and as such it is necessarily and eminently concrete. The problem is simply that thought is unable to catch and freeze-frame it in order to discard it and immediately move over to

---

[22] See Barthes, *The Neutral,* 190.

another opinion. Doxa simply hates the neuter, but the feeling is mutual.

Some say that this neuter is therefore useless because it always already comes with the oppositions that make language comprehensible. Its complexity prevents it from being politically 'useful,' for example. The problem really is that the neuter remains both *borne* by the whole language (and therefore describable and useful *as such*) *and* that which, amidst oppositions, *never* enters language properly (and therefore remains always difficult to describe or use *as such*). The neuter is therefore both useful and useless. The political is doxa's sister and therefore harbours more or less the same feelings towards the neuter.

SEXED AND GENDERED

However strange this might seem, especially if one considers this afternoon's hard-on, this neuter is what carries no mark of opposition (against the female sex or women, for example). The issue here is that in common language, the very word 'neuter' usually implies, as seen above, a reference to a binary opposition: neuter versus masculine and feminine, for example. The problem is that *this* neuter cannot be submitted to or positioned against such binary poles. It remains with both at all times and yet never belongs properly to one or the other. The neuter is improper, but even that is not its property.

However, this neuter should not therefore be understood as a paradoxical prototype for the human, a type of sexlessness or a 'genderless thing.' It is not an 'us,' an indifferent 'nobody and everybody,' or an a-phallic and a-cephallic generic state somewhat mysteriously recognizable across the bumpy plurality of bodies. The neuter is the primordial complex positivity that takes place *before* sexuality and gender. In other words, this neuter is a decisive positivity that comes *before* the specification of sex and gender as binaries.[23]

---

[23] The idea of a primordial positivity is inspired by, but departs significantly from, Heidegger's interpretation of Dasein's neutrality.

Primordial? Before? Uh?

This neuter must indeed be understood as preceding any form of dichotomies or bi-polar (a)symmetries. This precedence is due to the fact that the neuter cancels the one and outnumbers the two and as such *precedes* both the one and the two (neither/nor, masculine/feminine, male/female, etc.). In other words, it precedes because it is a positivity that knows no different. It is that which comes 'before' binaries.

However, the 'before' in question here is a curious one. However much, it appears to indicate a period of time that precedes another, however much it gives the impression that there is an order of priority, this 'before' must be understood, following Jacques Derrida, in a situation that knows no literal, chronological, historical, or logical meaning.[24] The 'before' in question here simply means what disperses sexual difference and the difference of sexes and genders as bi-polar (a)symmetries.

In this way, this neuter is not a rejection of sex or gender, the negation of the feminine and the masculine, for example. It is the positive dispersion of sex and gender. This neuter disperses its own sex, which here, for example, happens to be male. In this way, this neuter disperses this morning's

---

The reasons for departing in such a way from Heidegger's original formulation is simple: the argument about the neuter is neither attached to nor dependent on Dasein, that is, to an understanding of man as a being for which its own proper mode of being is not indifferent. The neuter is here analysed precisely as a characteristic of what is not neutral, that is, of what is always already contaminated by the other. The neuter concerns a 'with' (*cum*) that knows no unicity or directionality. For Heidegger's argument on the neutrality of Dasein, see: Martin Heidegger, *The Metaphysical Foundations of Logic*, trans. M. Heim (Indiana University Press, 1984), 136–40.

[24] Jacques Derrida uses the word 'prior.' See Jacques Derrida and Christie V. McDonald, "Choreographies," *Diacritics* 12, no. 2 (Summer 1982): 74. See also Derrida's commentary on this priority, especially in relation to space (making the difference between spacing and space as extension) in Jacques Derrida, "*Geschlecht*: Sexual Difference, Ontological Difference," *Research in Phenomenology* 13, no. 1 (1983): 77.

hardness, the needy weightiness of its scrotum, or any other erogenous or non-erogenous part of this very body. Preceding binary sex and gender, this neuter therefore 'positives' itself and in the process leaves hallucinatory projections and desires that postulates it as this or that (masculine or feminine, for example) to the economy of binary sex.

Such a weird precedence shows that the neuter is the event that baffles paradigms, and first amongst many, the sexual paradigm. It baffles because it is a positivity that never manages to fall back, yet again, into anatomical, biological or anthropological determinations. It is what invents (sexual and gender) determinations and hence can only leave the one that disperses them baffled, bewildered or perplexed as to why he is so determined.

All this has a terribly annoying consequence: the neuter and the masculine can no longer be seen as synonymous. This neuter does not stand for a specific sex or gender. It is not a secret substitute for men or a stable referent and its positivity is not a power or a violation of the other. No women are subjected *here* under a parody of (male) universality. On the contrary, this neuter is the start of sexes and genders even though it can never be identified as a starting point or an origin as such.

DISPERSION

While it lounges there in the afternoon sun slowly rousing from sleep, with its 22 pairs of chromosomes and its two extra set: X and Y; this neuter thus positively disperses itself. This is a pre-differential dispersion, a pre-sexual dispersion, or to be more precise, the primordial positive dispersion of the body 'before' its sexual and gendered determination in concrete form. This does not mean that, as dispersion, it is recognizable as a unitary, homogeneous, or undifferentiated proto-event: 'an in-born or in-herent neutral dispersal,' for example.

Coinciding with the advent of space and time, this neuter positively spaces (and) temporizes itself in its dispersion.[25] This dispersing therefore starts not here or there, but from the fact of being with others. It disperses itself as it sheds skin, its nails grow, its skin sags and as 'all this' comes in contact with others in the great dusty, sweaty, clammy maelstrom of humanity. The neuter is the slow dispersal 'towards' the other and the night—and this, even when the sun is still high.

As remarked above, this dispersion curiously knows no language and yet it forms and is formed by language. This neuter, this spacing (and) temporizing, indeed disperses at the moment when, as language, this 'origin' submits to its law. In other words, this neuter spaces (and) temporizes itself just when language imposes the weighty rule that makes it comprehensible as a neuter. In this way, although it is a 'start,' this neuter never escapes the laws of language, hence the fact that it can still be (more or less) articulated.

But, and this will annoy even more, there is therefore no way of understanding this dispersion as if it were a 'work,' like the work of the negative, for example. There is no labour, operation, or performance here, and there is no negation or opposition. This neuter positively disperses and always displaces itself out of its dispersal, thus making it impossible to ascribe it a proper ground, course, centre or reversal as such.

But how is one, finally and to finish, to make sense of this odd 'positivity' that does not even have the politeness

---

[25] As I have done in my previous books, *On Futurity* and *After 'Rwanda'*, and following the observation adhered to in the Introduction, I make a distinction between space and time and spacing (and) temporizing, with the latter's conjunction always bracketed. The former refers to measurable space and time and therefore to things that lend themselves to mathematical calculations and historical interpretation. The latter refers to the radical unhinging of space and time, *as far as language permits us to hear it*. For the words 'spacing' and 'temporizing' in Derrida's work, see: Jacques Derrida, *Speech and Phenomena*, trans. D.B. Allison (Evanston: Northwestern University Press, 1979), 143. For a commentary on this topic, see Françoise Dastur, *Telling Time, Sketch of a Phenomenological Chronology*, trans. E. Bullard (London: Athlone Press, 2000), 13 and 105 nn. 43 and 44.

of remaining constant and therefore recognizable by all as something lovely and positive?

As its etymology clearly states: 'positivity' means what is placed or what occupies place (*ponere*) and yet this 'occupancy' takes place without a clear indication of placement, location, or position. It capriciously posits itself without adopting a final position, let alone a final disposition. In this way, this neuter positively places itself as it de-places itself. This does not mean that it is just a frustrating protean ghost. This simply means that in order to 'be,' the neuter almost never ceases to visibly show itself in order to remain at the cusp of visibility. Even the negation of the neuter exscribes[26] itself in the process; hence the fact that it is a positivity that isn't a power or a powerlessness, a potency or an impotence.[27]

This neuter is therefore not 'what exists' here and now. Complex, the neuter is messy and messes around; it misses a step and yet still manages to step in time. As such, it can never be reduced to a single signifying and reductive term ('life,' for example), copula ('be,' for example) or, as we have

---

[26] I use again here Jean-Luc Nancy's famous word in order to emphasize how this positivity works. However, the use of such a word is always made with Nancy's careful warning: "'Exscribe' is not a word in our language, and one cannot invent it (as I have done here) and remain unscathed by its barbarism. The word 'exscribed' exscribes nothing and writes nothing; it makes a clumsy gesture to indicate what can only be written, in the always uncertain thought of language": Nancy, *The Birth to Presence*, 339.

[27] Again, the difficulty here is to think a positive dispersal that is not pitched against a negative one. The use of the word 'positivity' therefore necessitates a situation in which the antagonisms (sex, gender, etc.) are already in play. Positivity thus becomes what sustains the antagonisms or oppositions as if the very condition of their existence. As such, the neuter's positivity is that which constitutes the divides positive/negative, masculine/feminine, etc., but without the possibility of 'a backwards glance' because it is an unpredictable surge that knows no tide, earth, or moon. For an analysis of these problems, see Peggy Kamuf, "Derrida and Gender: the Other Sexual Difference," in *Jacques Derrida and the Humanities: A Critical Reader*, ed. Tom Cohen (Cambridge: Cambridge University Press, 2001), especially 100–4.

seen, a standard operational device for existence ('Dasein,' for example); one that would give meaning or direction to the economy of subjects and objects, me, you, it, they. This neuter maddeningly smudges and disarranges copulas, correlations, and clever devices mercurially remaining at their cusp.

In this way, even in its own complex disarray, this neuter still evokes a movement, but this movement is not as straightforward as it seems. Because it coincides with the 'origin' of space and time, because it fuses itself with a concrete sexed and gendered bodily reality, this neuter is really—however odd this sounds—the positive 'not yet' of factual dispersion. This 'not yet' is not what can be recognized as coming but isn't here yet. This 'not yet' is also not a pregnancy, potentiality, or futurity and however odd this sounds, the 'not' in this positive 'not yet' relates to no negativity or radicality. It simply marks the way the body goes about to positively disperse itself—we will come back to this. For the moment, let us simply say that the neuter as the positive 'not yet' of factual dispersion is really a complex bestrewal without surface. There would be no man (and more generally no body) lying there in the sun without it.

2. Sexual Difference

Dispersing, I become a sexed body. The 'sexed' in question here only concerns the body 'prior' to its forced classification into a bio-anthropological or ontic determination (male, man, for example). Once again, this 'prior' is neither chronological nor logical. A sexed body simply refers to a body that has at least 'a' sex. Whether I recognize it (and therefore use it) or not is here as yet to be determined.

Similarly, the 'I' referred to here is not yet an entity recognizable as such; it is only a random number of indefinite disseminations surprisingly arriving at multiple points at the same time to say 'you.'[28] No specific unity, whether empirical, subjectal, or nominal, can be identified here. The saying in question is simply a puzzling happenstance that language only manages to recognize with an inadequate and reductive 'I.'[29]

---

[28] This is a reformulation of Gayatri Chakravorty Spivak's famous sentence in: Gayatri Chakravorty Spivak, "Love Me, Love My Ombre, Elle," *Diacritics* 14, no. 4 (Winter 1984): 28.

[29] As Rosi Braidotti rightly says, "The power of synthesis of the 'I' is a grammatical necessity, a theoretical fiction that holds together the collection of differing layers, the integrated fragments of the

As this dispersing sexed body, 'I' experience something unprecedented: a caress. This caress is not masturbatory yet. The hand hasn't reached the erection; the mind is still elsewhere. This caress is that taking place between parts of the body: a bicep by the ribcage or an open hand peacefully resting on a breathing stomach, for example.

How am I to understand this event that necessarily involves a sexed body but occurs 'before' language determines its gendered performance and sexuality takes hold of its phantasmagorical grip? This will be the topic of this next step in the exploration of this particular masculinity.

Please note: the following text makes a distinction between sexual difference and the difference of sexes. While the latter emphasizes a bio-anthropological opposition (man/woman, for example), the former highlights an indefinite number of sexes all taking place in one body and, specifically here, in this dispersing sexed[30] body. In this way, there will be in *this* chapter no reference to the classical difference that biological sex and socio-cultural   gender always entails, but to an arrangement[31]

---

ever-receding horizon of my identity": Rosi Braidotti, "The Politics of Ontological Difference," in *Between Feminism and Psychoanalysis*, ed. Teresa Brennan (London: Routledge, 1993), 93.

[30] Because we are here 'prior' to the forced classification of man into a distinctive bio-anthropological or ontic determination, the non-bio-logical noun 'sex' or adjective 'sexed' can therefore only be understood with split or open words like, for example: im-proper (never quite mine), im-pure (never quite clean), or in-decent (never quite honourable). These words are more or less detached from a biological referent and yet remain at the cusp of intelligibility, that is, necessarily and as this body never tires to remind me, a-logical.

[31] I use the term arrangement and not assemblage in order to avoid the kinds of (Deleuzian) assemblages put forward, for example, by Jasbi K. Puar. The reason I prefer arrangement to assemblage is because it allow for 'what cannot be known, seen or heard' (to use Puar's words) to come and disrupt it: i.e. make a mess of the arrangement. The worry I have with Puar's assemblage is that 'what cannot be known, seen or heard' must be incorporated within the assemblage as yet another 'network' thus running the risk of creating a new totalizing narrative ultimately called a (Deleuzian) assemblage. With arrangement, my

known as sexual difference, an arrangement that, as will become clear, only a caress can make sense of.[32]

As will be explored, this arrangement is conceived following the work of at least one author: Emmanuel Levinas and one of his most careful readers: Catherine Chalier. The reason for this choice is as follows: When it comes to sexual difference

---

aim is to think how 'what cannot be known, seen or heard' actually de-structures the issue without necessarily appropriating it as part of the structure. Furthermore, to think this should avoid easily going from 'being' to 'becoming(s)' and thus remaining stuck within a Deleuzian paradigm that, ultimately, only displaces the problem without taking the law of absolute heteronomy seriously enough. This law—and here I can only go against Puar's argument—does not bring forth waves of the future breaking into the present. To say that it does can only effectively reassert and reinvigorate the singularity and dominance of the 'I' that Puar so forcefully rejects because, *as always*, this very 'I' remains *secretly conceived as being stronger than time* and thus able *'to see'*—with Puar in tow—how the "future break into the present." For Puar's thought-provoking essay, see: Jasbir K. Puar, "Queer Times, Queer Assemblages," *Social Text* 23, nos. 3-4 (Autumn-Winter 2005): 121–39.

[32] As it must be self-evident by now (and as it will become clear later on in this chapter with terms such as arrangement, impropriety, perpendicular dislocation, and irretrievable remainder), the event sought here under the heading 'Sexual Difference' cannot be understood as an a-priori transcendental abstraction detached from concrete bio-ontical sexual realities. Although it occurs 'prior to' the difference of sexes, the event of sexual difference cannot be seen to found the difference of sexes. Conversely, although the difference of sexes happens 'after' sexual difference, it cannot be seen to result from it. In a situation where there is no formal logic, there can be no hierarchy or order of priority (temporal or otherwise). Sexual difference is not an empty floating signifier and the difference of sexes is not its concrete content. The two necessarily contaminate each other without altogether forming a couple as such. No understanding of the body can take place outside of all abstraction and vice versa: no abstraction can take place detached from its concrete (or bodily) origin. For a fruitful discussion on this topic see the conversation that took place between Judith Butler, Ernesto Laclau, and Slavoj Zizek, in *Contingency, Hegemony, Universality: Contemporary Dialogues on the Left* (London: Verso, 2000), especially Butler, 144–8, Laclau, 190–2, and Zizek, 256–8.

(and not the difference of sexes), Derrida leaves us with an unruly but unsatisfactory "choreography of sexual voices."[33] It is unsatisfactory, because it never deals with the dynamics of the choreography. Who hears what and how in this dance? Re-reading Levinas helps us to see that this choreography is in fact structured as—and this is precisely what will remain to be shown in this chapter—a perpendicular dislocation that knows no rest.

Please also note that the following chapter does not pretend to put forward yet another general theory of sexual difference for the human race.[34] As should be clear by now, the sexual difference in question here is only that of *this* sexed body lying here on the ground. Any generalisation taken out of the following descriptions can only betray its specificity and, as is well known, can only be disloyal to its own fabulation.[35]

---

[33] "I have felt the necessity for a chorus, for a choreographic text with polysexual signatures.... The relationship would not be a-sexual, far from it, but would be sexual otherwise: beyond the binary difference that governs the decorum of all codes, beyond the opposition feminine/masculine, beyond bi-sexuality as well, beyond 'homosexuality' and 'heterosexuality' which come to the same thing. As I dream of saving the chance that this question offers I would like to believe in the multiplicity of sexually marked voices": Derrida "Choreographies," 76.

[34] And for this reason, I will therefore shamelessly refrain from thinking this bio-graphy in relation to the animal realm. The reason for such shamelessness (*cette pudeur* to recall Derrida's cat) is to prevent any attempt to think 'beyond' oppositional binaries (man-woman, human-animal) because, as is well known, such attempt can only lead us either back to the same (man, for example) or into an unwieldy infinite plurality. Oppositional binaries need to be thought otherwise and this is what is attempted here. For how sexual difference relates to animal difference see: Jacques Derrida, *The Animal That Therefore I Am [More to Follow]*, trans. D. Wills, *Critical Inquiry* 28, no. 2 (2002): 369–418. For a commentary on such a relation, see Kelly Oliver, "Sexual Difference, Animal Difference: Derrida and Difference Worthy of its Name," *Hypatia* 24, no. 2 (Spring, 2009): 290–312.

[35] As Jacques Derrida says: "If I were to say 'sexual difference is a fable,' the copula 'is' would permit the proposition to be turned around: a fable, thus every fable, is sexual difference, which can be understood in many ways. We can say that every fabulous narrative recounts

MASCULINE-FEMININE

As is well known, sexual difference, like the neuter, must be thought outside of any form of opposition. When sexual difference is determined by opposition in the dialectical sense, there is no choice, but to misinterpret sexual difference, confuse it with the difference of sexes, and set off once again the famous war between the sexes thus inevitably precipitating the end with a victory going to the male sex and men in general.[36]

In this way, the terms 'masculine' and 'feminine' are not used here in a way that is reducible to a member of the male or female sex. In other words, the feminine does not equate to woman and the masculine does not equate to man. However much this will infuriate those who cannot open the word bio-logy, the terms masculine and feminine will be used here as logical improprieties within the positive neuter of this body. An impropriety is simply what never accords with itself: being masculine is never my own and yet I recognize my masculinity.

When I was a child, I had long hippy hair and people often thought that I was a girl. Even when I was an adolescent, when I more consciously opted for long hair, I was also deemed to be more feminine than masculine. I lacked virile qualities. This didn't annoy me; it simply puzzled me. Even then, I thought that whoever or whatever I was, I could only be an odd juxtaposition of masculine and feminine.

---

sexual difference, stages it, teaches it or offers it for interpretation; or that 'fable,' that is to say, speech or parable, *is* all of sexual difference. Sexual difference, if there were such a thing, would be fabulous. There would be no speech, no word, no talking that would not say and would not be and would not institute or would not translate something like sexual difference, this fabulous sexual difference. And there would be no sexual difference that would not go through speech, thus through the word *fable*": Jacques Derrida, "Fourmis: Lectures de la différence sexuelle," trans. E. Prenowitz, in *Rootprints: Memory and Life Writing*, ed. Hélène Cixous and Mireille Calle-Gruber (London: Routledge, 1997), 120.

[36] See Jacques Derrida, *Glas*, trans. J.P. Leavey, Jr. and R. Rand (Lincoln: University of Nebraska Press, 1986), especially 4–5. See also Gayatri Chakravorty Spivak, "Glas-piece," *Diacritics* 7, no. 3 (1977): 22–45.

Now that I have grown up, I realise that the masculine 'in me' is not due to the possession of a penis, but that it is a way of ap-propriating my'self' and ultimately has nothing to do with sexuality or gender. The feminine 'in me' de-propriates[37] such foolish attempt at property with as much force or strength as that expressed by my masculinity. The play between the two occurs not as a fight between opposite forces, but as the necessity of being both, that is, improperly complex.

In this way, and as will become clear, a) the masculine and the feminine are not single and autonomous regions or aspects of the body, b) they do not come in sequence, c) they do not obey an order of priority, and d) they are not equal or comparable entities. As previously stated, the masculine and the feminine are here understood as an arrangement of improprieties that *this* specific body could never ap-propriate/de-propriate fully or with any clarity.[38]

Sexual difference is therefore not to be thought of as a straightforward opposition or hierarchy between masculine and feminine or between the active mastery of a subject and its passive submission, but rather as the necessity of having to be a 'sexed' body with all the various improprieties (masculine, feminine, etc.) that structure it and dispute for attention. In other words, sexual difference is the necessity of being a 'sexed' body in a situation where the word 'sex' always already remains to be invented.

---

[37] I transform here Heidegger's noun 'de-propriation' and make it into a verb: 'to de-propriate.' The verb does not exactly designate the self-withdrawal of being (*Enteignung*), but the precipitous action of destabilizing being. For Heidegger's noun, see: Martin Heidegger, *On Being and Time*, trans. J. Stambaugh (Chicago: University of Chicago Press, 2002), 23.

[38] I thereby adhere here to Derrida's understanding of sexual difference: "If 'sexual difference is to be interpreted, to be deciphered, to be decoded, to be read, it cannot be seen. Readable, thus invisible, the object of testimony and not of proof—and in the same stroke problematic, mobile, not assured": Derrida, "Fourmis," 121.

ECSTASY

The necessity of having to be a 'sexed' body (participating as the masculine and the feminine before these are transformed into opposed bio-anthropological entities) implies emphasizing an enigmatic bodily advent: the ecstasy (of) spacing (and) temporizing that structures this sexed body.[39]

At the heart or on the surface of this sexed body, there is a sexual difference that never ceases to be different and this whatever 'I' think and whatever 'I' do. This sexual difference is always already to-come and therefore necessarily on the edge of representation. As such, and however much two terms are used (masculine, feminine) sexual difference is, as previously stated, without recourse to formal logic or order, for it is always futural—hence the fact that it is an impropriety.

However, this sexual difference does not imply that there is 'something' autonomous that is recognizable as such: 'my (always renewed) sexual difference,' for example. The lack of referent means that sexual difference cannot be understood within the prism of a synchronic 'moment.' If this were possible, then I would automatically reduce 'it' to an instant (a longish second that would allow me to gather my thoughts and write a phrase, for example) through which I would recognize myself as either this or that; a recognition that would take place within a teleological order where the masculine would inevitably come first and the feminine last.

In order for it to escape logic properly, the sexual difference of this body cannot be 'a moment' *in* space and time. The absolute heteronomy (or diachrony[40]) that dislocates space

---

[39] Although the following draws its inspiration from the remarkable work of Catherine Chalier, it also attempts to gently depart from it. The aim of doing so is to simply rethink the relation with the radically other, a relation that remains in Chalier's reading of Levinas still untainted by language. For Chalier's main argument on this topic, see: Catherine Chalier, "L'Extase du Temps," in *Figures du Feminin* (Paris: Des Femmes: Antoinette Fouque, 2006), 137–70.

[40] I use here the word diachrony as a substitute for this law of absolute heteronomy and as a contrast to synchrony. Synchrony reduces time

and time also dislocates sexual difference. Inversely, sexual difference is what breaks space and time apart, a breaking that can never be understood as a breakage. In other words, sexual difference is the body falling out of phase with its sex, 'just as' spacing (and) temporizing disjoins space and time.[41]

But, if this is the case, then how can this diachronic sexual difference that appears to structure my sexed body be envisaged, let alone translated into words neatly arranged on this page? In other words, how can sexual difference be understood without glossing over its radical 'entanglement' with the law of absolute heteronomy? Let me return and expand on the positive 'not yet' of factual dispersion mentioned in the preceding chapter on the neuter. This return and expansion will unreasonably flirt with bodily allusions, but these, as will be shown, should never be taken literally.

---

to space and always ends up with a conception of time and space that is measured and homogeneous: an (in)finite series of punctual moments spread along the axes of past (present) and future, for example. Synchrony is the time of the Said to use Levinas's vocabulary. By contrast, diachrony is, as we have seen in the Introduction with regards to heterogeneous time, what breaks time and space apart. It is the falling out of phase with itself. Diachrony is the time of the Saying. The contrast created between synchrony and diachrony does not however exclude ana-chrony, which is what is without foundation or origin. For a concise analysis of these issues see: Emmanuel Levinas, "Jacques Derrida: Wholly Otherwise," in *Proper Names*, trans. M. Smith (Stanford: Stanford University Press, 1996), 59.

[41] This can be extended—an extension that I deliberately avoid doing here in order to limit the scope—to the entry of the subject as a breaker of space (and) time. Joan Copjec explores this quite remarkably in her essay "The Sexual Compact." She writes, for example: "The crucial point is this: Freud gives sexuality the same structure that he gives to the temporality of psychic functioning. This relation is not founded on mere analogy; neither term—time or sex—has priority over the other. The two are co-originary. The subject is sexuated inasmuch as she is finite, subject to time. Or: sex belongs not to the essence of the subject but to her historicity; it defines her life of pleasure/unpleasure inasmuch as she is finite, subject to time's vicissitudes": Joan Copjec, "The Sexual Compact," *Angelaki: Journal of the Theoretical Humanities* 17, no. 2 (2012): 37.

'BETWEEN'

Dispersion necessarily implies horizontality, a spreading or a distribution over a period of space and time. As such, it is also a deployment of language. As a deployment, it is essentially masculine, it disseminates, it is seminal, it has something to do with emissions, which are also forms of emptying. This does not equate language with being male or a man. When the masculine is understood as an impropriety 'within' the positive neuter of this 'sexed' body, the deployment of language knows no gender.

Sliding down perpendicularly,[42] dispersion *also* implies verticality, a fact that creates intervals and therefore allows for the deployment. As such, it is also a disruption of language. As a disruption, it is essentially feminine; it falls or descends thus marking space and time, which is also a way of creating the world. As such, it has something to do with cycles, which are also forms of timely uncertainties. Once again, this does not equate the disruption of language with being female or a woman. Similarly, this feminine disruption of language knows no gender.

---

[42] I have no competence here to link or relate this perpendicular structure to that envisaged by scientists (for example, that developed by Hermann Minkowski and later by Albert Einstein). The idea of perpendicularity simply comes from reading a passing remark in Eberhard Gruber's text on Levinas's understanding of sexuality: "Autrement que sexuellement marqué? Lecture d'Emmanuel Levinas," *Literature* 142 (June 2006): 57, my translation: "What does then Levinas understand by 'relationship'? He perceives it as a temporal crisscrossing: the time that 'splits the terms of the relation' is subordinated to diachronic time. One could judge the feminine as being far too close to reality to signify the (human) condition of *withdrawal*, this symbolic charge that is usually understood as masculine because unable to give birth. But what matters is that this logical thinking of the withdrawal … is that of a diachronic thinking, which allows one to situate the masculine and the feminine not in opposition or in complementarity, but in a perpendicular relation. The vertical line would be what is 'before,' while the horizontal line highlights a 'succession.'"

This intervallic fall and this interrupted deployment create a kind of 'between' spacing (and) temporizing that can never be identified, measured, or weighed. This 'between' is neither a juncture (an 'and' that can be heard), nor, more metaphorically, the place of bisexuality or hermaphrodism, for example. This 'between' is a *rapport* of horizontality and verticality that never manages to *report* back, let alone make sense as such. If it did, then it would be nothing other than a fold created by divine agency. Instead, it is the 'between' birth and death, the union-separation[43] involved in any happenstance.

This 'between' obviously takes place 'after' the neuter, but still before any spatial or temporal and therefore 'before' any bio-anthropo-logical and historical determination. Once again, 'before' and 'after' do not refer here to an order of priority. This 'between' occurs 'before,' that is, it 'carries' (itself *with*) the factuality of being male or female, a man or woman. As such, it can never be understood as a negative force. Of the same order as the neuter, the 'between' created by this vertical slide and this horizontal deployment can never be rendered dialectical, be sublated, or deconstructed because it always evades a fixed point from which this could happen.

---

[43] I follow here Nancy's work, albeit with a slight divergence. Ian James provides the clearest summary of Nancy's understanding of the body when he writes: "[Nancy's] thinking of the corporeal as an event at the limit of sense, as an opening or spacing of discrete places, is seen in terms of a rupturing or fracture, or what Nancy will call an 'effraction,' within two types of continuity, that of sense and that of matter." Nancy's rupturing, fracture, or effraction is close to the 'between,' 'union-separation,' or 'logical absurdity' that I develop in this book (and in *After 'Rwanda'*). However, unlike Nancy, I situate this effraction not 'within' the historical continuity of sense and matter, but right in the spacing (and) temporizing that provokes the historical event of sense and matter. For James's quote, see: Ian James, *The Fragmentary Demand: An Introduction to the Philosophy of Jean-Luc Nancy* (Stanford: Stanford University Press, 2006), 131.

A PERPENDICULAR DISLOCATION

The crucial aspect of this 'between' 'prior' to measured space and time is that it allows one to situate the masculine and the feminine not in opposition or complementarily, but in a perpendicular dislocation in which the masculine and the feminine dislocate themselves 'just as' spacing (and) temporizing disjoin space and time.

This perpendicular dislocation knows no co- (and as such cannot be seen as a correlation) that would form a secret commonality or 'togetherness' between the masculine and the feminine or a subject and object, for example. What is perpendicular never forms 'two.' The fracture brought on by absolute heteronomy can know no relation. If it did, one would be in a synchronic moment, that is, *at* a specific moment in space and time, relating this and that together.

This perpendicular dislocation can therefore never be seen as that which is connected, associated, tied-up, or joined together. It is perpendicular because, like diachrony, it is the spacing (and) temporizing of that which occupies space and time, without ever letting itself be recognized as an 'expression' of spacing and/or temporizing, for example.

The fortunate or tragic aspect of this perpendicular dislocation is indeed the fact that it can never be recuperated by memory or history (and thus forced into a dialectical relation productive of narratives and myths like that afflicting poor Oedipus and Electra). The dislocation of the masculine and the feminine occurs every second of time anew, strange, unexpected, vexatiously alienating: the evermore-unexpected ruin of memory and history.

Although two improprieties have been singled out here (masculine, feminine), these are not exclusive or representative of sexual difference. Others, subtler, more imaginative, or simply to-come could have been chosen to expose such a perpendicular and always futural dislocation. Sexual difference is not a given; dislocation always lies ahead (if it really were given, one would have a relation of dislocated 'items' floating in space and time, and no one would want that and this, even if, clarity is the least of our concerns).

AN IRRETRIEVABLE REMAINDER

However, notwithstanding the empirical indistinguishability between spacing (and) temporizing and sexual difference, there appears to be a transcendental distinction between the two. This distinction is the fact that unlike diachrony 'as such,' sexual difference can only be an irretrievable remainder[44]: what remains of diachrony—qua diachrony.

Once again, this remainder precedes measurable space and linear time and therefore is allergic to memory and history. Before the subject, before the difference of sexes understood as male and female, man and woman, this remainder traverses this positive neuter body without ever being or becoming a remnant, appendage, protuberance, or prosthesis that can then be translated as an identity, an essence, or excrescence to the body.

This remainder makes thought go on endlessly and will never allow itself to be thought out properly. It is that which is always already on the fore front of this mind but never lets itself be grasped or figured, not even before sex (being horny, for example) and certainly not after an orgasm (being alleviated and elated, for example). Like the dislocation of space and time, the remainder or sexual difference can never stop or be stopped and this, even when in a coma or in the grips of senility.

---

[44] This irretrievable remainder echoes Jean-Luc Nancy's interpretation of the sexual as the supernumerary or surplus of the body. However, although it echoes this interpretation, it also divests itself from it because the remainder of this chapter stays with sexual difference and not the difference of sexes. For Jean-Luc Nancy's interpretation see: Jean-Luc Nancy, *58 Indices sur le corps et Extension de l'âme* (Quebec: Nota Bene, 2004), 66 and Ginette Michaud's commentary on this surplus in "Appendice," 85–122, especially, 110–16. The translation of Nancy's text can be found in Nancy, *Corpus*, 160.

SUBSTITUTABILITY AND THE UNEXPECTED

The curious thing about this remainder or sexual difference is that it cannot be understood, as Catherine Malabou rightly observes, outside of substitutability.[45] The masculine, the feminine, or any other impropriety can change from one into the other at any time. This does not mean that within the body they remain the same and swap places occasionally. Substitutability does not mean replacement. Improprieties have no ability to fix themselves in space and time. There would be no 'between' without substitution.

However, this is not a self-contained or self-enclosed system that would perpetually modify itself as if some ever-malleable self-contained plastic toy or inventive drag queen or king. Absolute heteronomy plays a curious part in this substitutability: it indeed digs out the spacing (and) temporizing in question here, right in the flesh of difference. This crucial role avoids treating the masculine and the feminine as general and generic forces locked in a mutual embrace or at war. Absolute heteronomy disrupts the game, always making an opening for the event or the performance of any one of these improprieties.

Inevitably, in the same way that sexual difference is allergic to synchronic grammar, it also cannot be regulated by any kind of subjective, objective, natural, or civil law. At the mercy of absolute heteronomy and a player in this very heteronomy, this substitutability expresses the positive madness of sexual difference. It is 'mad' because resolutely out of control and this whether I live the recluse life of an abstinent monk or spend my time getting drunk, shagging, and/or cross-dressing.

---

[45] I follow here Catherine Malabou. However, as the next paragraph shows, I slightly alter her interpretation of substitutability, thus making it less Hegelian. For Malabou's remarkable observation about substitutability, see: Catherine Malabou, *Changing Difference: The Feminist and the Question of Philosophy*, trans. C. Shread (London: Polity, 2011), 37.

CARESS-BEFORE-TOUCH

And this is how I happen to caress myself, lying there half-asleep, in a slumber. My bicep touches my side. My hand rests on my downy stomach. Such contacts express a myriad of different modes of othering my sex, the remainder of the ecstasy (of) spacing (and) temporizing. Neither strictly masculine nor feminine, my male body caresses itself; thus breaking space and time: digging out or opening up a new or unfamiliar impropriety.

At no point can I pin down a moment in this caress. It always leads me to another moment, another repose open to the contingent. In the grips of heterogeneous time, this para-doxically controlled and uncontrolled 'movement' has no specific sexual attributes (a typically male kind of stroke, for example). It leads me astray without altogether getting me lost.

As such, this caress cannot fall under the sense of touch, contact, or sensation, which will be explored in the last chapter of this book within the context of the difference of sexes. What is caressed here is really not touched.[46] A movement that carries itself out is beyond the realm of the senses because it is necessarily futural: it does not know where it is going and as such marks the dusk of being, the ebb of knowledge, the wane of light.

In this way, the caress in question here can only be a movement of exteriorization that cannot be gathered, a move-ment that exceeds itself without there being an inside or an outside to this excess: blind experience. The bicep and the hand are still. The two exceed themselves beyond their very

---

[46] I obviously borrow this idea from Levinas. However, unlike Levinas and after him Derrida, I deliberately refrain form confusing this type of caress with that taking place in the context of the difference of sexes. In other words, Eros here is not yet awake. On this familiar Levinasian theme, see Emmanuel Levinas, *Totality and Infinity: An Essay on Exteriority*, trans. A. Lingis (Pittsburgh: Duquesne University Press, 1969), especially 260–1; and Derrida's reading of Levinas's *Time and the Other* in Jacques Derrida, *On Touching Jean-Luc Nancy*, trans. C. Irizarry (Stanford: Stanford University Press, 2005), 77 and n. 17.

singularity, right at the moment when the body abandons its mastery, recedes from being-able and shivers or shimmers with unforeseeable possibilities.

In this way, this caress or excess awakes a sexual difference that no new caress or excess can appease. No shift of the body, no move of the hand can bring any sense or relief to this sexual difference. In its stillness, this sexed body thus remains open to a new event, a new mode of being or tendency—the unexpected breaking apart of space and time, a spacing (and) temporizing that never affords a pause or a poised attitude.

This positive madness of sexual difference—which allows for this substitutability between the masculine and the feminine or any (other) improper perpendicular dislocation—rules this caress. It is a ruling without power or authority and yet, however contradictory this sounds, always already in the hands of a conscious decision: remaining horizontal, not moving, in a slumber.

The crucial aspect of this madness is that it is really the only thing that allows me to evade the overwhelming violence of indistinctiveness that being 'me' here on this simple straw mat implies. In other words, the caress provokes in me a forgetting of being, that is, a letting-go of the weight and the horror of being reducible to just 'one,' 'male,' 'a man' (even if this 'one' is always indefinitely withdrawn further away). The ever-unfulfilled or always renewed caress relieves me from these singular and autocratic confines.

Through this forgetting of being, the caress therefore allows me to open a future that is different from that of (my) death. We will come back to this. For the moment, let us say simply that my open hand peacefully resting on the hair on my stomach or my bicep gently touching my side implies a space and time other than that of my death; it intimates the other of the masculine, the feminine, or of any other impropriety; an other that no prediction or projection can possibly envisage. To caress is indeed to unsettle without ever mastering 'it' the perpendicular ecstasy of spacing (and) temporizing.

3. Male

INTRODUCTION

He almost falls back to sleep.[47] The 'he' in question here is the echo of the previous 'I.' A 'he' always comes after a first person pronoun, once an 'I' is heard—which does not mean that this 'I' has been recognized or identified. 'He' is the pronoun of representations and narratives. At the risk of being accused of illeism, the 'he' in this chapter will echo the 'I' because representation is the only tool available to make sense of what cannot be talked about: my resting male body.[48]

---

[47] Suffering from insomnia, sleep in this chapter will not refer to the state in which the nervous system is inactive and consciousness suspended, but to a state of drowsiness or somnolent watchfulness, the sense of being 'there' and yet unable to fully grasp what this 'there' actually means.

[48] As Jean-Luc Nancy says, when I sleep, "I no longer properly distinguish myself from the world or from others, from my own body or form my mind either. For I can no longer hold anything as an object, as a perception or a thought, without this very thing making itself felt as being *at the same time* myself and something other than myself": Jean-Luc Nancy, *The Fall of Sleep,* trans. C. Mandell (Stanford: Stanford University Press, 2009), 7.

In his slumber, he is able to seek refuge from the never-ending task of always attempting to compose himself, to take action, and being someone. In other words, with rest, he gives up the task of always seizing himself in order to fight for his place in the sun in this exiguous present that is never present enough, never accomplished, never totalised. His rest allows him a relief from this exhausting, and, alas, at times, violent task.

Dozing off is thus more than simple rest from alertness and war. Besides being a moment of recuperation, sleep, however light, is also the manifestation of a suspicion towards the limits that appear to structure him and his day. In other words, with a nap, the suspicion is expressed that the fight might not be entirely necessary, that the exiguity of the present might not be as real as it seems. Sleep is the suspicion *of* being.

However, even this refuge is not entirely peaceful. He drifts off with the covert or blanketed knowledge that a hand will perhaps rouse him, even arouse him, thus forcing him to abandon his refuge and return to the laborious day-task of articulating and positioning himself in the world. He thus rests knowing that the suspicion *of* being is only temporary, that the violence of being knows no real refuge, except death.

But this other hand isn't there yet. In his or her temporary absence, this male body reveals himself in all its vulnerability. How is one to think this exhibition of maleness? If the masculine—as previously defined—is the deployment of language, then how does this deployment manifests itself in this display of *maleness* and how does this *male* body relate to the feminine interrupting him every second of time? These will be the questions of this third chapter.

Two main authors will help to address them. These two authors are careful readers of Levinas, but who interestingly, diverge in their reading of his work: Catherine Chalier and Luce Irigaray. The latter arguably inaugurated the now classic reading of Levinas as a misogynous philosopher. Irigaray's aim is to avoid not only reducing women to alter-egos of men, but also to alert to the danger in Levinas's work of allowing the feminine to stand for alterity. Catherine Chalier, by contrast, takes up this juxtaposition of alterity and the feminine in order to continue throwing into question the dominant masculine modes of thinking that permeates western philosophy. For Chalier, the feminine as alterity, on the contrary, ruptures (male) ontological categories. The divergences are clear and the following text will attempt to negotiate them as (un-)faithfully as possible.

Please note that although the following chapter focuses on the male body, there will be only dangerously tangential references in what follows to the gender known as man as opposed to woman. The male body retains here as its intrinsic characteristic the fact that it is neuter and both masculine and feminine as previously defined. Male here means the incredulity of being a man not because of an unwillingness to believe in the condition of being a man, but because of the impossibility of ascribing a property to what is called 'man.'

The word 'incredulity' does not imply an event, like, for example, 'He *now* doubts that he is a man.' Incredulity ex-poses itself over time; it ex-hibits itself as a historical narrative without discernable beginning or end. In this way, his body ex-poses that it will 'always already' be incredulous that he is a man or that 'man' is indeed his property—or a property as such.

Please also note that some people will not recognize in what follows a male body. Those—men or women—who think that a male body is only truly representative if it comes in the shape of sweaty fighters, skilled action heroes, brave warriors, iron-willed bodybuilders, or airbrushed supermodels will simply be disappointed. This is the male body, as it is not supposed to be seen.

THE MASTER

He is now resting and yet, when he will be fully awake, he will immediately fall into a cliché: however much he dislikes it, his body will stand for what society expects it to stand for: a male who, because he is male, necessarily masters language (being strong, for example). He will be the one who in his body is 'naturally' unconstrained by language: the master, or so he will hope to be (and so does, when it is convenient, the rest of the human race).

With such power and freedom, he will take his body to work. At work, his body will use a language that constantly confirms his stability and mastery. In the process, he will further stabilize his body by associating himself with other terms such as vigour, power, potential, virility, phallus, authority, etc. He's all guts and balls, changing his life, changing the world, for good or worse—more often than not, for good *and* worse.

Something else will also happen: while looking, his body will conquer and objectify (he apparently knows no other way of looking: an unfortunate impediment of his sight). Through this taking and possessing, his body will thus becoming invisible, un-representable. His body will be all eyes, objectifying the world from an unshakable seat of power: his ocular centrism, a position that knows no proper rival.

However, having such a stable base and referent has a price: he cannot articulate his body otherwise than in relation to a scrutinized and projected (idealised or not) opposite: a fragile, feeble, or vulnerable body. In one word, his ('invisible') body will be dependent on what ('visibly') is not 'pure-eyes': a female body. He will indeed not only define his body as this opposite, but he will also articulate his body in the necessary dependency of this opposite: he will be male because he desires and/or rejects female bodies, thus helping him being who he imagines he ought to be.

This price has a curious consequence: however much he longs for independence, he can never achieve it. His body will always already be dependent on an other body (for example, the body of a feeble and mannered ubiquitous poofter) who will also never be able to be independent. The chain of dependency will always be infinite. However much he hates it, his grasp of his body will remain always already shaky and indefinite, never properly accomplished or perfectly hollowed out, never entirely asserted or erased.

In this way, however much his body will struggle to be the master of language, this very body cannot allow him to be secure, the day-work will always have to be re-started, the fight for mastery will have to be directed, this time, against other bodies, other real or imaginary powers or weaknesses. Never, will his body allow him to escape the demands of being such a cliché (but then, maybe this is the fate of all bodies).

This is not a defeatist thought: 'boys will be boys,' or 'he's just a bloke, really'—thus vindicating the cliché. This simply means that however much the pressure is on, the grasp of the male body is always already uncertain. The cliché is *never always* properly accomplished. The fight thankfully *never always* properly won. (What always needs to be fought is the *fall* into the cliché, the *abdication* to the delusions created by biological fate.)

THE SENSIBLE

And yet, here he is, lying there in the sun. His body is open to examination: He is passive, fragile, vulnerable, and exposed. Since he is outdoors, his skin is exposed to the fiery sun, his body is vulnerable to the winds coming form the sea. There is an over-abundance of exposed maleness here that is curiously ready for representation, that is, possession.

As such, he is not quite the one who masterly represents; he is no longer the subject, the lord of theory and concepts, pure eyes. He is here, most simply, the sensible, a vulnerable significant phenomena, a non-ideal chaos of corporeal being. As this sensual body, he is thus anterior to the violence of representation and to violence full stop: an unusual state for a male.

Currently failing in his task of trying to be the master, this male body cannot therefore present himself in terms of sameness and representation. He is not the self-present or the self-evident. This does not mean that, while he is suspicious of being, he is the outside of presence or the other of representation, for example. He is here simply, and in the most relaxed manner possible, failing mastery. His supposed power over representation is here clearly lacking.

However much he cannot escape *properly* the demands of being a cliché, this cliché paradoxically does not therefore always apply. This male body here has none of the attributes usually associated with (virile) male bodies. He is here most simply an empirical beginning. While he will never be maternal, he can at least be here matrical:[49] he *provides* for representation; he is a *gift* for representation.

MORPHOLOGY

Here are a few recklessly chosen examples of how he can be a gift for representation:

First, inevitably (for where else can one start?), he has a penis (that joker[50]) and a scrotum. These protuberances are

---

[49] There is no space here to explore the theme of the matrix or the matrical as a (male) empirical beginning. Suffice to say that the matrical is not understood here as something in space and therefore as something visibly attributable to women only. The matrical is the giving of space and time; a giving or providing that knows no gender strictly speaking. As such, I distance myself here from the remarkable work of Irina Aristarkhova who writes most eloquently on the theme of the matrix and the maternal. The reason I distance myself from this work is simply because the matrix or the matrical cannot for me be understood within a measured spatial and temporal framework and consequently be limited to biological or cultural references. For more on this a-gendered matrix, see Jean-Paul Martinon, *After "Rwanda,"* (Amsterdam: Rodopi, 2013), especially chapter 2, "Matrix - Akantu." For Aristarkhova's work, see Irina Aristarkhova, *Hospitality of the Matrix: Philosophy, Biomedicine, and Culture* (New York: Columbia University Press, 2012), especially, chapter 2, "Materializing Hospitality."

[50] "When it comes to the naked male form, the penis is the joker: it is that which cannot be represented because of its ability to veer the representation into pornography, it is what is improper to representation": Jean-Luc Nancy and Federico Ferrari, *Nus sommes (La peau des images)* (Brussels: Yves Gevaert, 2002), 68, my translation.

supposed to prove that a male body is not only invisible, but also, paradoxically, visible to itself. A man or a woman can look down and see that indeed he is male. Nothing is here hidden. All is in plain view, nothing evades representation; everything is morphologically emphatic.[51] Nakedness never stares back.

This familiar interpretation of the male body, as that which is visible to itself, implies an absurd reduction of the male body: a monolithic and monologic economy with a few protuberances. As is well known, the male body is more than this apparent visibility, which at times gets hidden on a surgical table or under a roll of fat.

Second, the reversed myth that the male body is always already visible to itself obscures the fact that this male body lying here is also easily penetrable. He moves in his sleep and the between of his legs offers a penetrability, which he himself cannot see. This is a contrary aperture, but an aperture nonetheless, a darkness that easily bleeds at any violent intrusiveness.

This penetrability unexpectedly transforms the male body into a dwelling, a dangerous supplementary welcome par excellence. As such and however unusual this may sound; this male body becomes an open interiority that cannot be appropriated; a 'hospitality' before any form of sociality; a natural and yet contrary supplement—if one can say such a thing.

Finally, his obvious visibility clearly shows that his body is unable to bear children. This does not mean that he is infertile. This simply means that *he can never be two*—we will come back to this. This confines him to this world of representation and to this endless struggle of mastery, the athletic and yet pathetic commonplace effort of being.

---

[51] As a radical counterpoint and as an inevitably unwise step aside into the realm of sexuality, see, for example, the persistent and problematic *figuration* of lesbianism as unrepresentable, invisible, and impossible in Annamarie Jagose, *Inconsequence: Lesbian Representation and the Logic of Sexual Sequence* (New York: Cornell University Press, 2002).

ESCHATOLOGY

His fertile and yet barren situation gives him an unusual attribute: he is eschatology itself; he is the end of man. This does not mean that he is a genetic dead-end or that he alone stands for eschatology, as if some symbolic walking end. He is the end because however much the feminine interrupts his body perpendicularly every second of time, his male body forces him to be *above all* the deployment that leads to the end.

In other words, being 'sexed,' and his sex being male, gives him no other choice, but to embody the end. His bodily deployment 'speaks' of the end. This 'speech' is not an ability to express thoughts and feelings by articulate sounds. This 'speech' is that expressed by his always-lonesome male body. If he didn't have this mediating 'speech,' his body would be dead matter.

Although he can play at being the messiah and project into the future, he can never be *properly* messianic: he can never be the beginning of man, for example. He can only be messianic by proxy. Never 'two,' his male body simply prevents him from opening the future with another 'one.' Confined to distance, mediation, representation and therefore ends, he can only deploy the end—eschatology.

In this way, while the (fecund) female body tears humankind out of history with her children and therefore into a hereto-unheard future, this male body can only take himself and others into the future conceived teleologically, that is, as the outcome of accumulated past and future presents. This is his lonesome task: deploy for himself and others the end. In this way, this male body is simply—a simplicity that often pains him—the laborious finality of history.

Unable to give birth and therefore always an origin at a distance—a metaphorical distance for it can also be the sultriest of intimacies—his inextricable eschatological confine puts him in an always uncomfortable double bind:

Firstly, his body is a call to fiction. This call is directed to the *female body* and this whether he is 'heterosexual,' 'homosexual' or 'queer.' The fact of the origin is unknown to him because always already mediated, imagined, represented. This does not a) equate the female body with fiction, b) elevate the female body over the male body, or c) give the female body a privileged knowledge; this is simply the recognition of an inevitable bodily call to fiction about the facticity of origin.

Secondly, his body is also a plea to women to extend himself beyond death. Never two, he (in most cases, a 'heterosexual' 'he') longs to meet a woman who can give birth to 'his' child, a child that, *at a distance*, will take him, whether he likes it or not, somewhat beyond death. Once again, this does not elevate the female body or women in general as the sole provider of a life beyond finitude. This is simply the recognition of a lonesome plea to be taken out of eschatology.

This call to fiction and, for some, this plea to women shows that although his body is condemned to be eschatological, he is not just for death; he is also for a beyond death. In other words, while his body can never tear mankind out of history, his efforts at being the laborious finality of history is also paradoxically an effort to be (together) the laborious infinity of history. Eschatology is never one-sided, providing, of course, one can recognize a side to eschatology.

NO HERO

Notwithstanding his often-aggressive pride in his maleness—masculine deployment does not always translate well in the male body—he is thus an alienated being. Even his day-time work will not be able to overcome this: He will always remain alienated not only by the 'other' (as un/defined in the Introduction) but also by the products he creates, these manly tools that always end up rising up against him, always untamed and hostile, mere symbols of his end of history.

Even when he is seen (supposedly) mastering his existence and his products (the media bombard us enough with such delusory images), his eschatology still prevents him from being a hero. He can be no hero *properly* because death still holds him in its grip. Death indeed remains (even for him, who stands for the end) a 'never now,' something that will always already evade his eschatological grasp. In front of the great reaper, he is effectively a weakling, like anybody else.

The male body lying here in the afternoon sun is therefore clearly no hero because as soon as he will awake, he will always already hope not to die: death will simply come to him, eventually, the final submission to time. And even if he plans to commit suicide, he will still be unable to master death; he will simply succumb to it because of his inability to carry over to the other side his mastery.

THE APPEAL TO THE FEMININE

Hence his never acknowledged appeal to the feminine, which *here, in this context,* is *not* a call to the female body as his eschatological salvation *or* a plea to woman as his bio-anthropological opposite, the potential mother to 'his' child. This is a different kind of appeal in comparison to the previous two because it is not, as we have seen, relational, but perpendicular.

As stated before, in (or all over) this male body lying here in a slumber, the feminine and the *un-mediated* future coincide in a coincidence that knows no incidence. In this way, his appeal to the feminine is an appeal to the future, to what comes from above, takes his breath away, and marks (and therefore allows for) his singular lonesome and finite deployment. How is one to understand this appeal (which is also, paradoxically, an appeal to self)?

In his intractable solitude, this male body finds himself bound to and by an indefinite present. Within this present, he is breathless: he is always already trying to find a solid base from which to assert himself. Unfortunately, however much he tries, he remains stuck precariously in this indefinite, but finite present: between an inherited past that always eventually vanishes into the immemorial and an always-mediated future that always seems to come from nowhere.

And so he turns, for want of a better solution, to what he thinks is the 'instant present': trying to live 'it' as much as he can: young, working and partying hard, old, enjoying the moments that come knowing the end is near. In each case, he exposes an always failing sovereignty, a lack of mastery over a time that is never really his. This failing mastery is the only result possible when the instant present (past-present or future-present) is sought out.

The only way he might be able to overcome such failing is if he finally acknowledges his appeal to the feminine. The perpendicular fall of the feminine—this fall that gives him his confining present—is indeed the only 'thing' or the only 'one' that can allow him to escape the fatality that structures and overwhelms him in the present: his eschatology.

Unsurprisingly, the recognition of this appeal is *not* what will finally tame once and for all his endless propensity to master himself. The acknowledgement of this appeal only allows him to relax a little, that is, to accept that his body *is* also this feminine fall that both makes possible and alleviates his end-game—a strange kind of acceptance, an odd taming of mastery because it is the exact opposite of becoming effeminate.

To become effeminate is indeed to dismiss the body's eschatological confine; it is to pretend that a male body can potentially or momentarily open the future. While the act of becoming effeminate is a valid endeavour; it unfortunately can never entirely overcome its limit: the end of man. Saying this does not imply calling for a return to an archaic virility, but for a sustained questioning of improprieties (masculine and feminine) all in the aim of taming mastery—and this, even if dresses are being worn.

Once a little tamed, he will then perhaps be able to *stop* grasping his body only to stupidly shatter it against death, haughty and proud: the vainglory achievements of *man*-folk. If this taming ever happens, then this male body will perhaps begin to take time to be against death, to postpone it, procrastinate, have patience. If this taming ever happens, then this male body will perhaps also begin to signify otherwise, that is, at the same time, in an impossible simultaneity, otherwise than being[52]—a difficult task that is far from being achieved.

But hush, this male body is slowly stirring, turning over, progressively regaining consciousness, growing grumpier as he awakes: the need for mastery steadily clenching 'its' grip. This slow turn reveals his many sides, angular, hairy, robust, smelly, warm, delicate, graceful. An abyss in every crevice, a mass at every turn, this male body can reach neither a plenitude of meaning nor a truly stable referent. His language, like his body, betrays him at every turn: never quite masculine, ever more virile/effeminate, never enough feminine.

---

[52] The intention here is not to put forward an easy philosophical quip that would pretend to overcome in one single brushstroke Levinas's outstanding argument in *Otherwise than Being*. The intention here has its roots in a previous book where the juxtaposition of the violent (male) 'being otherwise' and the ethical (feminine) 'otherwise than being' are analysed at length. See *After 'Rwanda,'* particularly chapters 5 and 6.

4. The Side Story

INTRODUCTION

The story goes that he is a man and that he is profoundly asleep, that is, in a sleep that nothing, not even a knife to his side would awake. We do not yet know who this man is. One thing is certain: he definitely does not stand for humanity; he is just another man, maybe the wrong man.

With this story *comes* a woman. Unlike he, who is fast asleep, she is awakening, slowly gaining awareness of her strange surroundings. We also do not know who this woman is. Maybe she stands for kindness, or maybe she is simply another woman. She too is perhaps the wrong woman.

In the following chapter, there is a difference of tense. His side of the story is told in the past tense, while her side is more or less transcribed using the future anterior, this compound tense that consists of two verbs: an auxiliary verb in the *future* tense ('will') and a *past* participle verb ('have read,' for example). 'More or less transcribed,' because although facticity needs no explanation, language nearly always fails to transcribe it, commentary always creeping in, unnecessary and yet, however annoying, unavoidable.

In any case, the future anterior is the only tense available. There would be no 'side' story (and therefore no fiction in general), if it were not for this crucial temporal tense that expresses the im-possible factuality of the (living) present by gracefully resting on both past and future ('will' 'have...').[53] In other words, without this tense, that is, without the factual emphasis implied in this compound tense, there would be no fiction, explanation, or commentary.

This chapter has two aims:

The first one is to demonstrate—once more, can this be done enough times?—that the origin of all things has, contrary to Aristophanes[54] and the authors of the Bible,[55] neither an androgyne nor a lonely man as a starting point, but a couple[56]

---

[53] I follow here a well-known Derridean use of tense. As Simon Critchley explains: "The significance of the future anterior is that it is a temporality irreducible to what Derrida would call the 'metaphysics of presence' or what Levinas would call 'ontology,' and one which envisages a language that would escape the dominant interpretation": Simon Critchley, *The Ethics of Deconstruction: Derrida and Levinas* (Edinburgh: Edinburgh University Press, 1999), 115–6. See also, Diane Moira Duncan *The Pre-Text of Ethics: On Derrida and Levinas* (Bern: Peter Lang, 2001), 156.

[54] Plato, *Symposium*, trans. W. Hamilton (London: Penguin, 1951), 58–66.

[55] Genesis 2:22–24.

[56] The following is inspired by, but also departs from, a commentary by Jean-Luc Nancy in a series of notes written for a seminar at the University of Paris 8 on 28 January 2005 and subsequently published in *Littérature*. The commentary is as follows: "If one must wait for something out of the division of sex (this division of the one-being narrated in Aristophanes' discourse in the Banquet) it would have to be that One (from which two supposedly appears) never really existed. The conclusion would be that the division would have always preceded it. And if this is the case, then there is never division or separation. The division is therefore the originary relation, the originary exposition, and this must also be understood as the original exposure itself: if the origin 'is' relation, then the origin dissipates itself in the relation": Jean-Luc Nancy, "Et après," *Littérature* 2, no. 142 (June 2006): 34, my translation.

and that it is impossible to think about this masculinity, male body, and man without thinking this supposedly originary couple, which defies all kinds of nostalgia for unity.[57]

The second aim of this chapter is that this couple brings fact and fiction together: a fiction about an inversion of biological truth and a biological fact that can only be expressed using the future anterior. The unusual aspect of this juxtaposition is that neither fiction nor fact can be understood independently of each other.[58]

Please note that his side of the story is told here first. This does not show the usual disrespect or a contradiction in the

---

[57] Always desperate to dominate, always in need to control, aimlessly wondering alone in their own superiority, male readers of Luce Irigaray's recent work (*In the Beginning, She Was*) can only be left at once in awe and disturbed at her discourse. *The End of Man* will not be addressing the contents of Irigaray's latest work. The reasons for not addressing this important late book is this: Although it takes 148 pages for Irigaray to admit that, she is "not a male person," the whole book is structured on the basis of a gross generalization about men: what they are like, have always been, and presumably will always be. Women on the contrary are either (understandably) the victim of men's oppressive language or (curiously) elevated to such a degree that it is no longer possible to differentiate between "she," "the goddess," and "Mother Nature"; the last holding men (and women) as if in a perpetual womb. Irigaray's curiously phallic discourse relies heavily (however much she decries it) on an unflinching Hegelian hetero-normative dialectic in which women and men are placed, without ambiguity, in radical opposition to each other, an opposition that ultimately can only be sublated when a self-affected, but mysteriously undefined "we" pops up (on the last page) finally recognizing its common origin in this all-encompassing "Mother Nature" (tsunamis and earthquakes presumably included). How does "Mother Nature" come about, is not explained, but "we" must allow her—or Her—to emerge in order to stop sexism, misogyny, and patriarchy. See Luce Irigaray, *In the Beginning, She Was* (London: Bloomsbury, 2013).

[58] This does not mean that fiction and facticity are the necessary components of every reality or that they are eternal. Fiction is not necessarily fabrication. It is also invention. Facticity is not necessarily a fact. It is also the possibility of disputation. In both cases, it is impossible to talk, as Meillassoux intimates, for example, of an implicit

chapter. Fiction can only come first because this is *her* story. Consequently, the subsequent transcription of the fact can only be made here, *by me,* fraudulently. The relationship between hermeneutics and facticity can only indeed be fraudulent because a fact—and the fact of giving birth specifically—is not something that one can take cognizance of or have knowledge about, not even while holding the hand in a maternity ward. Facticity is an existential knowing.

Please also note that any similarity with fictitious or factual events or characters is purely coincidental. The reading of texts such as *The Bible* (especially Genesis 2:4-2:25), Mieke Bal's "Sexuality, Sin, and Sorrow," Daniel Boyarin's "The Politics of Biblical Narratology," and the texts of Phyllis Trible are not necessarily accurate. Following a Talmudic tradition that Levinas never tires to recall, what counts above all is not the truth of the texts examined, but their reading. Texts are not here to be studied as if dead matter, but in order to contribute to their message and this implies, in a gesture that can only be as respectful and faithful as possible, to create misreadings all in the hope of pushing things along and thus contributing to the Word. As Levinas says, pushing the argument way further: "the irreplaceable part that every person and every moment contribute to the message—or to the prescription itself— which is received and whose wealth is thereby revealed only in the pluralism of persons and generations."[59]

FICTION

Once upon a time, there was a man lying down in a pool of sun, sleeping. Except for his sex, no specific features marked him out. He was simply a naked man lying down presumably

---

absolutization. For lack of space, I leave this enormous question in suspension. For a challenging discussion of these issues, see Quentin Meillassoux, *After Finitude: An Essay on the Necessity of Contingency,* trans. R. Brassier (London: Continuum, 2008), especially chapter 3.

[59] Emmanuel Levinas, "Foreword," in *Beyond the Verse,* trans. G.D. Mole (London: Continuum, 2007), xvi.

on some grass, in a garden among trees, doing nothing, but napping.

Of course, he was breathing and his heart was beating, but he had no control over them. His hairy chest went up and down and his heart pumped blood, but without any controlling gesture on his part. He occasionally snored, but even this did not manage to wake him. It was as if someone else was in control of the task of taking air in and out of his lungs and of pumping blood in his heart.

Lying there in the sun, he was thus unable to refer to himself and therefore to assert himself against another (God or nature, for example). He was clearly without referent and therefore without power. Even his penis was here useless. He was just mere matter, a lump of breathing flesh.

This lack of control was in fact quite remarkable because at one point that morning (or afternoon?), part of his side disappeared. This drastic event took place without sedatives. Suddenly and without interruption to his snoring, his side was wrenched out of him. He clearly was not mastering his body.

But this was not all; he was also unable to control whomever was subsequently created from his side. He played no role in the creation made of his flesh and bones. He was neither a participant nor an observer. He just slept.

And yet, by having his bones and flesh wrenched out of him while he slept, he also paradoxically became in the process 'for the other.' He was not just separated from a part of himself; he also became 'for the other,' a kind of generous inability to hold it together, a gift without mastery or control (an ironic 'start' for what later will always strive for mastery and control).

However this gift was not meant as an altruistic gesture. His loss of flesh and bone was an in-voluntary gift made to whoever was created out of him. This gift was a little unusual for it evaded all forms of economy: it expected no return for he, himself, was without return.

As such, this was his own form of maternity. Yes, maternity and not paternity for here no conception at a distance took place. There was no arousal, penetration, and ejaculation in the hope of conception, gestation, and birth. He un-wittingly gave himself in his sleep or more precisely, he un-intentionally brought another to the light of day.

Some will say that this is a strange kind of maternity because it more or less coincided with the birth of his ability to speak and therefore with his ability to wage war. However, such coincidence might have something to do with it. After all, through his side gift, he not only gave himself away, he also opened up the possibility of disputation and therefore war. Unfortunately, there can be no maternity without war.

However, such a gift was not an indication that he was either the first or the only one at the start of creation. Teleology here means nothing. Neither cause nor purpose, not even a random series of events can structure such a happenstance. The surreal parting of some flesh without suffering or anaesthetic clearly places the event in question here outside of all logic. If this were not the case, there would be neither fiction (the (re)telling of this or other story) nor facticity (the suffering of birth) in the world.

Two then started the world. The 'two' here is what is in question; it stands for the impossibility of the question, like, for example: Was I snoring? Did you sleep well? Did you have nightmares about bleeding to death? These questions are impossible because their answers necessitate both facticity and fiction *before* the invention or creation of facticity and fiction: a glorious aporia that knows no poros. In this way, space and time have no origin *properly speaking*; they open each other to create an interruptive doubt or ambiguity about origins, wakefulness, and bad dreams.

After much repetitive snoring, he finally woke up. The woman by his side asked him a question. He replied by remaining silent, obedient. He did what he was told for she had awakened *first* and already knew the ways of the world. She later gave him fruit, which he ate in silence.

The end.

FACT

She will have been *first*. She will have been the first to recognize herself not only as a human being awakening one afternoon, but also, considering the man snoring by her side, as woman. In doing so, she will have given him the possibility of also recognizing himself. The birth of subjectivity will have come from her, first.

She will have also been the bearer of another gift: Her refusal to bow down to the authority coming from on high (a refusal that, as is well known, demonstrates will, autonomy, and thoughtfulness) will have given him the power of knowledge. (Suddenly, apples are not the only fruit.)

(These two first gifts show that the process was in fact relatively fair: 'two' giving each other: on the one hand, as it were, flesh and bones, and on the other, self-recognition and knowledge: an odd, but perfect equity—which does not mean equality—the separation of what comes together: flesh and word).

However, although their birth took place in perfect equity, there will also have been (at least...) four main discrepancies (the history of the world is paved with all the others):

Firstly, for good or bad (and although she was the first to be named), she will have given him the opportunity to be the first to speak (*first discrepancy*). (Insolent, he grabbed the opportunity unceremoniously: the first to signify. His first speech could have been: 'after you, madam,'[60] but no...). In

---

[60] I deliberately (and perhaps a little perversely) reference here Levinas's famous attempt to address the ethical through the sentence: 'after you, sir.' The aim here again is not gratuitous. The aim is simply to highlight that even as fiction (Adam's parting rib story), the ultimate ethical gesture of giveness (Adam's giving himself away) cannot be distinguished from the economy (and therefore the violence) that comes with the act of giving (Adam's first speech). For Levinas's reference, see: Emmanuel Levinas, *Otherwise than Being*, trans. A. Lingis (Pittsburgh: Duquesne University Press, 2004), 186; Emmanuel Levinas, *Ethics and Infinity, Conversations with Philippe Nemo*, trans.

doing so, she will have suddenly become 'the other character.' (As the character who spoke second, she was often then 'spoken to.' This, as it should always be emphasized, had disastrous consequences).

But this will not have been all; in the process (*second discrepancy*), she will have also managed to turn God into a character. (As a *nameable* entity, God thus came third in the 'suddenly' teleological order imposed by language. Such a low ranking position meant that He would never be able to regain His powers as 'original' potter and midwife, thus remaining for ever a mere topic of conversation and a(n) (un)reasonable addressee for prayers—with all the unfortunate consequences that this position entails—being supposedly neutral, the third party, the judge...)

Third discrepancy: having introduced these two characters, she will have also introduced, in the process, the fictional story summarised above: this story of rupture: the surreal fiction of man's parting side, parting without origin, immemorial. (Unfortunately, as is sadly known, those who interpreted it grossly misread it. They—men, obviously—were convinced that they once were able to give birth from their side, thus giving them the delusion of thinking themselves closer to God... As is well known, patriarchy partly rests on a misreading).

Finally (as if giving him the opportunity to be the first to speak, turning God into a fictional character or witness, and introducing the fiction above was not enough), she will have added a *fourth discrepancy*: she will have kept childbirth to herself. (No more side-parting for him. Being 'for the other'—*epekeina tes ousias*—should always be seen—whether as fiction or fact—as a gendered affair). As compensation, she will have given him the shared experience of both sexual difference (masculine-feminine) and the difference of sexes (male-female, man-woman). (For good or bad, they tend to make the most of this).

R.A. Cohen (Pittsburgh: Duquesne University Press, 2004), 89; and Emmanuel Levinas, *The Time of the Nations*, trans. M.B. Smith (London: Continuum, 2007), 97.

(But this last discrepancy was not entirely egoistical:) By retaining the ability to give birth to herself, she will have also given them both the seemingly endless possibility of change. (They now occupy historical positions: being a son-becoming-father and a daughter-becoming-mother. Together, they make history.)

The beginning.

A QUESTIONING

What is one to make of this juxtaposition of fiction and facticity, the latter being more or less comprehensible with the use of the future anterior? What does this inversion of biological truth (the fiction of 'a' man giving birth to a woman) and this biological fact (the facticity of 'a' woman giving away subjectivity, knowledge, speech, fiction, and babies) tells us?

The meeting of fiction and facticity shows that each protagonist constitutes him or herself not in order to form a whole, but in separation. They are together as separation,[61] a strange kind of status that never coheres either as a lovely story (turning a rib into a woman makes surrealist stories somewhat second rate) or as a comprehensible event (birth is, after all, always a miraculous fact).

As such, they will always already be unable, not to be whole in a Platonic sense, but to totalise themselves. The meeting of facticity (woman's birthing comprehensible only through the use of the future anterior) and fiction (man's chronological story narrated in the past tense) is a meeting that leaves them (man and woman) unable to perceive themselves as singular

---

[61] I explore this expression in detail in *After 'Rwanda.'* I borrow this expression from Derrida who writes: "Face to face with the other within a glance and a speech which both maintain distance and interrupt all totalities, this being together as separation [*cet être ensemble comme séparation*] precedes or exceeds society, collectivity, community": Jacques Derrida, "Violence and Metaphysics: An Essay on the Thought of Emmanuel Levinas," trans. A. Bass, in *Writing and Difference* (London: Routledge, 2001), 119, my emphasis.

meaningful entities (either as a singular moment *in* space and time or as what is always already *outside* of space and time).

In this way, their sex, like their lives, is always already 'not yet.' Man and woman are, each time, another man and woman, another experience, another life. Hence the fact that they could always be the wrong guys: they never are in the right place, always already elsewhere. In this way, He and She are always already futural and yet curiously unable to predict the future.

Thus man and woman are not just better or worse halves to each other; they are always already equivocal, always open to interpretation: at once clearly defined and recognizable as such and yet never absolutely cogent or coherent: each one expecting the other to make sense of their being together as the sense of their togetherness separates them away. With *and* without the other, they cannot live.

Thus, when they play, they are simultaneously always already in need (past repeating itself as present) and desire (the present projecting itself as future), a muddle of fact and fiction ruled by a mixture of concupiscence and transcendence that keeps them together as separation: the enigmatic as such.

However, this fiction and this facticity are not everything. In their equivocalness, they are still mortal, vulnerable, and sensitive; neither man nor woman is eternal and, as the cliché goes, that is precisely the only thing they have in common: the fact of being born and dying—mortal neuters with sexes.

This finite nature brings eschatology (man 'never-two') and messianism (woman 'sometimes-two') together. This togetherness, as we have seen, is not a cosy work in tandem or a necessary correlation, but a union-separation that is irreducible to any traditional form of reading or logic of representation: being together as separation.

Considering such an odd situation, their task, should they accept it, would then be to provide each other with what they ought to give away: an end to the story (man), the beginning of the story (woman). Their task is therefore not to seek union or fusion, but to maintain together their separation. Each ending and each beginning validating and cancelling each other thus making them 'be' a little longer still.

This task is akin to love, because to love the other is to give what one does not have: the end, the beginning. Again, this does not mean that these will match, in the way one would imagine the end matching the beginning, for example. There is no eternal return here, not even of the type that recurs every second of time because love creates time indistinguishably as end and as beginning.

To give what one does not have is therefore to ensure that ends and beginnings, fact and fiction remain always already in play, in love. The task is to never overcome the duality 'man and woman' however much they try, however much it gets blurry, and however much they are always called upon at sunrise and sunset to hear that 'God is One.'

5. End(s) Meet

INTRODUCTION

Straying not far from the garden, I meet a man. The non-erotic caress that I originally experienced in my solitude before falling asleep suddenly acquires sense: directing itself this time towards this other. I now become aware of how touching him leads me to places I would have previously never imagined existing. In doing so, I now enter the realm of the difference of sexes.

To follow a Deleuzian vocabulary, this encounter shows that I have now become someone who, in his sexual comportment—a comportment that isn't unique—strives in the process to become inhuman.[62] I am not just a human being with a rigid sexual identity. As I touch this other man, I awake my body's intensities and surprise it by making it other to myself, that is, inhuman.

---

[62] Gilles Deleuze, *Negotiations, 1972-1990*, trans. M. Joughin (New York: Columbia University Press, 1995), 11.

The longing for this never-quite-attainable inhumanity shows that every time I have sex, I have a new sex. One new sex on each occasion. This shows that I can never precisely calculate the gift of my sexual life. My sexuality is always already in the order of the incalculable. There is nothing extraordinary about this. My sexuality is simply, like other sexualities, always already to-come.

Such a familiar openness to the future usually tends to obscure the end[63] of this particular form of sexuality: in my case, two men: the cum cloth (or any other means of discarding semen). Where is this sexuality going once both need and desire have been fulfilled? The answer to this question is usually the laundry basket: the place that holds the promise of another time, the possibility that the gesture will be repeated. But what does this repetition, which is also a promise, really stand for?

Understood more broadly, the question can perhaps be formulated in this way: Factually and in most cases, fecundity requires sexuality, but sexuality does not require fecundity. What end is then sought in a sexuality without the potential of fecundity? In other words, does this type of sexuality embody a type of eschatology that avoids—to speak in broad terms—any form of messianism: the meetings of (genetic) dead ends?

The aim of this chapter is to challenge the manner in which language (including queer theory[64]) ossifies us and delivers

---

[63] The end sought in this chapter is limited to sexuality. Ends such as 'being in love' and 'being in an amorous companionship,' for example, would necessitate another set of references and another vocabulary that, for lack of space, cannot be addressed here. For example (amongst others): Roland Barthes, *A Lover's Discourse: Fragments*, trans. R. Howard (London: Vintage, 2002).

[64] Queer theory ossifies us because it rarely acknowledges that the term 'queer' cannot be defined in advance. Queer should always be a term that resists hypostatization and reification into a proper nominal status. The only way queer theory can indeed retain its credibility as a tool for thought is if it always begins with this resistance against a definition. For such careful caution, see the Introduction to Carla Freccero, *Queer/Early/Modern* (Durham: Duke University Press, 2005).

us without us having our say, that is, without waiting for us to give birth to it. The aim is thus to invent new words and new ways of thinking in order once again to prevent language burying us—as always—too quickly.

Unsurprisingly, these new words do not originate out of the blue. They stem from other traditions and affiliations. One in particular will draw most of our attention: Emmanuel Levinas's understanding of fecundity, especially in the way Catherine Chalier's interprets it. There is no space here to expose Chalier's interpretation. Suffice to say that it significantly departs from the majority of scholarship on Levinas's fecundity in the way it takes the law of absolute heteronomy seriously. And this, as hopefully will be demonstrated in the following pages, helps give 'gay' sex a hereto unheard of future.

In accord with this different affiliation and the perspective taken in the Introduction, the following will inevitably not address the creation of different historical temporalities (or alternative 'chronotopes') in order to question or combat hetero-normative time, this 'reproductive futurism' that, according to Lee Edelman and others always associates the future with the figure of the child.[65] There are two reasons for this:

The radicality of heterogeneous time does not allow for the assertion that there is such a thing as a singular abstraction ('heterosexual,' 'homosexual' or 'queer,' for example) that can be isolated from a larger social matrix. However much one

---

[65] Once again, this is not intended as a pitch against queer theorists, but as an attempt to put under close scrutiny the problematic of the spatial and temporal dimension of sexual subjectivity; a dimension that, as stated in the Introduction cannot do away with the radical interruption brought upon by the law of absolute heterogeneity. For this reason, this chapter cannot address the remarkable issues raised by authors who are invested in creating non-linear and/or non-filiative temporal biopolitical subjectivities. For the most prominent of these authors, see Lee Edelman, *No Future: Queer Theory and the Death Drive* (Durham: Duke University Press, 2005) and Tim Dean, *Unlimited Intimacy: Reflections on the Subculture of Barebacking* (Chicago: University of Chicago Press, 2009). See also, Carla Freccero, "Fuck the Future," *GLQ: A Journal of Lesbian and Gay Studies* 12, no. 2 (2006): 332–4.

cannot really dispense from producing or inscribing lexical, cultural, social, or political differences, these in turn can never escape the possibility of being put into question. Through this ever-persisting questioning and the possibilities offered by answers, futurity then comes to light—and this is what will have to be shown in this chapter—as that which knows no discrimination.[66]

Secondly, and more generally, whether 'straight' or 'queer,' humanity does not seek to exclusively express itself by productions or inscriptions (of subjectivities), but by its approach to the other. In the context explored here, this approach, as will become evident, is only an attempt to evade (as much as possible) the oppressive tyranny of this 'I' that always seeks to gather itself into presence and representation ('*I* am a father' or '*I* am a bug-chaser,' for example) and *with* the other to always provoke, maintain, renew or push further our very inhumanity.

Please also note that the following will assume as a general principle that, notwithstanding modern reproductive techniques, a 'gay' erotic encounter does not usually lead to procreation. As such, men who seek sex with men do not *usually* seek to become parents. Those who do will probably not identify themselves in the following pages.

DEATH

Besides the fact that it can be washed, the soiled cum cloth embodies death. Washed, the future disappears amidst detergent and water down the drain. As such, this cloth exposes the inevitability of my death: there will be no more of 'me' in the future: 'me-as-other' stops there in the wash.

This particular end differs from that aimed at during masturbatory activities. These are performed (most of time,

---

[66] This does not exclude or negate, obviously, the possibility of creating futurities (queer or otherwise) for political purposes. For a remarkable example, see José Esteban Muñoz, *Cruising Utopia: The Then and There of Queer Futurity* (New York: New York University Press, 2009).

in solitude) as a form of relief from the tension imposed by testosterone. The end in this case is always already assumed in advance as self-evident. However much phantasmagorical characters populate the visual field and/or the imaginary, masturbation simply confirms solitude.

By contrast, in the amorous encounter in question here, what this (often shared) soft towel exposes is a deliberate act not only of emphasizing the importance of the present over the future, but also and above all of forbidding the future. There is a secret prescription that comes here in the activity that leads to this towel: the future is curtailed.

Happy with such a prescription, I live with and for my self and my death, even if this living takes place alongside another, in an amorous companionship, for example. In this way, each time I have sex, the unique, solitary, unchangeable, and extreme relation that exists with my death becomes exacerbated (and this even if I decide to 'acquire' children and/or pets and avoid at all cost saunas and backrooms).

I therefore live conscious of the fact that, unlike the majority of earthlings, I no longer possess an already predetermined or prescribed future. My scrotum is of no importance, only the penis counts (or here perhaps more specifically, only the phallus counts). Alone and valiant, I live without false pretences, such as believing in eternity or life after death, for example.

My erotic pleasures (and to some extent, my other forms of sociality) therefore always fail to open the future. The future remains for me exclusively that which comes with my possibility of no longer being-there. I live existentially (and, for some, socially and culturally) more than others precisely because of such lack of opening in my future.[67]

Let me return to this erotic encounter. The man I have just met caresses me until he founders in some orifice. In doing so, he does not attain 'communion' in view of someone else.

---

[67] Modern and contemporary literature and cinema swarm with examples of such 'high life,' from John Rechy's *City of Night* to Jonathan Kemp's *26* and from Frank Ripploh's *Taxi zum Klo* to Ana Kokkinos's *Head-On* to only mention arbitrary examples.

In this orifice, he only reaches the place where 'the feeling and the felt speak to each other.'[68] However, such speech is always already at a dead end.

The feeling and the felt go indeed so far as the vertigo can go. Neither he nor I lose our mastery and/or method, no biological mechanism is triggered and therefore no new birth can potentially come from that which is left either inside me or on my stomach. In this way and however adrenalized the occasion, our love-making is always already a return to the same—even if this same is here 'two.'

EROS

Let me now take some distance. However problematic it is to non-hetero-normative readings, 'heterosexual' erotic encounters are usually understood in pair with the concept of fecundity, in as much as they potentially promise the birth of a child. In other words, even when no children are sought, a 'heterosexual' encounter (even when it is mediated by a turkey baster or a clinical intermediary) is somehow always directed to the future via a potential fecundity.

The 'heterosexual' encounter is therefore an event of alterity; a relationship with what is absent at the very moment when everything appears to be there. In this way, the encounter takes the subject outside of itself, outside of the world of possessions and power. In doing so, the very structure of subjectivity changes as it encounters a dimension of futurity (the danger or the promise of a child) that is different from that of death.

In this way, the 'heterosexual' encounter is that which potentially can provoke an 'other' who, uniquely, can never

---

[68] I follow here—perhaps a little perversely—Luce Irigaray's argument, but with obvious different ends in mind. See Luce Irigaray, "The Fecundity of the Caress: A Reading of Levinas' *Totality and Infinity*," trans. C. Burke and G. Gill, in *Feminist Interpretations of Emmanuel Levinas*, ed. Tina Chanter (University Park: Pennsylvania State University Press, 2001), 122.

provide a return strictly speaking. By fulfilling this potential, the parents can thus eventually experience the fact of being both themselves and others to themselves. This is the only other *physical* relation to transcendence they will have besides death.[69]

The product of their sexual encounter—the child—thus introduces a multiplicity and therefore another future into the heart of the parents. With fecundity, a heterogeneity and a transcendence thus appear in the always mono-logic and monolithic verb 'to exist.'[70]

FECUNDITY

In this sense, fecundity is not so much a biological capacity to produce an offspring; it is also an escape or a way out of being (one). In other words, to have the ability to achieve the birth of a child comes in pair with a move beyond the biological. At an ontological level, fecundity thus opens one's mortality beyond any form of determined singularity.

This explains why fecundity neatly addresses the issue of a mortal life's meaning. A child is always a unique new beginning, a new responsibility to whom life can be handed over, continued, retrieved, amended, expiated, and to a certain degree, for some, fulfilled. This partly explains why engravings

---

[69] The type of transcendence exposed here can only be of a kind that cannot be lessened or appropriated. Our relationship to death is one such type of transcendence. The other is our relationship to the other and specifically here, to the child who, in most cases, will survive us beyond death. Emmanuel Levinas provides the clearest explanation for why this transcendence needs to be as radical as possible: "The unforeseeable character of the ultimate instant is not due to an empirical ignorance, to the limited horizon of our understanding, which a greater understanding would have been able to overcome. The unforeseeable character of death is due to the fact that it does not lie within any horizon. It is not open to grasp": Levinas, *Totality and Infinity*, 233.

[70] Emmanuel Levinas, *Ethics and Infinity, Conversations with Philippe Nemo*, trans. R.A. Cohen (Pittsburgh: Duquesne University Press, 2004), 72.

on tombstones are most often than not a marker of survival ('To Granny').

Furthermore, through fecundity, the child also stands for the continuation of the human race. In other words, the birth of a child is that which signifies a projection toward the future in terms of fulfilling a commandment that is older than history itself. This is the ethico-religious significance of fecundity, one that cannot be entirely dissociated from a mere existential or individualistic projection.

Finally, the relation between parents and child provides an 'account' of how humanity is overall produced: With a child, society, history, and therefore, overall, (homogeneous) *time itself* become exposed. In that sense, a child goes beyond the temporal immediacy of a historically localized encounter with another human being, a family, and a history to become 'that which' gives time.

At a banal level, this exposure or this givenness could be read as a confirmation once again of a hegemonic hetero-normative teleological structure or law. However, I'd rather read it here as a situation that does not imply the vapidity of a teleological evolution (have we not overcome this long ago?), but that of a meeting of always ex-ceeding ends: one end (father or mother) ex-ceeding itself onto and as an(other) end (the child) who is the same and yet altogether another (son/daughter – man/woman).

The child is thus not the commonplace evidential 'product' of a heteronormative construction of time, but like their parents, and before them, their forefathers and foremothers, an ungraspable property. By this I mean that neither the parent nor the child can be understood as self-contained subjects ready to be grasped as if they were 'properties,' but as ungraspable entities that de-propriate[71] themselves every second of time. In this way, the child is not the hegemonic

---

[71] I borrow again this expression from Heidegger. In his later work, Heidegger indeed looked for words that would indicate the event of Being otherwise. He chose, for example, the word 'disclosive appropri-ating Event' (*Ereignis*, from *ereignen*, 'appropriate,' and *eraeugen*, to see and disclose), which stands for a pure subjectless happening. He also

'emblem' of a conventional futurity, but what can never be reduced to a property and as such creates, like you or me, time, every time, anew.

THE SCHISM VIRILITY-PARENTING

Now how does this 'heterosexual' structure fare in comparison to my erotic encounter with this man? The issue is perhaps that in this specific embrace, a schism appears to take place in me.

This schism is not so much that between scrotum and penis (or phallus) as mentioned earlier, but more precisely, between parenting and virility, that is, here, specifically between my parental potential and my virile self—a schism here not exclusively conceived in biological terms.[72] How can I make sense of this schism of and in my subjectivity?

Virility usually implies the fact of having strength, energy, or a strong sex drive. Contrary to this commonplace assumption, I understand virility as the expression of a subject closed in on itself, a subject who is self-sufficient, pure self-possession. Closed in on itself, my virility therefore not only continually returns me to myself; it also transforms this self into an object.

---

chose the *noun* 'depropriation' or 'expropriation' as the self-withdrawal of being (*Enteignung*). See Heidegger, *On Being and Time*, 23.

[72] Many commentators accuse Levinas of understanding paternity in biological terms. As the following extract shows, paternity, as the opening of infinity, can clearly be conceived outside of biology: "The fact of seeing the possibilities of the other as your own possibilities, of being able to escape the closure of your identity and what is bestowed on you, towards something which is not bestowed on you and which nevertheless is yours—this is paternity. This future beyond my own being, this dimension constitutive of time, takes on a concrete content in paternity. It is not necessary that those who have no children see in this fact any depreciation whatever, biological filiality is only the first shape filiality takes; but one can very well conceive filiality as a relationship between human beings without the tie of biological kinship. One can have a paternal attitude with regard to the Other. To consider the Other as a son is precisely to establish with him those relations I call 'beyond the possible'": Levinas, *Ethics and Infinity*, 70.

Virile, I push myself and drag myself like a possession until I die and nothing will stop me in my path.

The consequence of this quasi-autistic self-possessed resoluteness forces the subject to relate to its future only as an endlessly re-affirmed power (even if it only encounters failures). Not even the other (male or female) in its weakness or magnanimity can interfere (let alone diminish or refrain) this re-affirmation.[73] The self-enclosure of the virile subject knows no other future, but its re-affirmation.

From the standpoint of the virile subject alone, the parent-child relationship can only therefore be understood as a conflict of wills, especially if it is—as is so often the case—confused with biological determinations such as paternity or fatherhood. Freud's notion of paternity, for example, makes the father-son relationship specifically a virile struggle for recognition in which the son must kill the father in order to inherit his recognition, designation, and power.

In contrast to virility, parenting frees the self from its self-enchainment and forces it to draw a line on this projection in order to open up to the other. Virility is the experience of the power of the subject, whereas parenting is the experience of the limit of the mastery of the subject. Parenting is therefore 'a fracture' in and of the virile subject. It breaks the obsessive self-sufficiency and self-possession of virility.

The parent-child relationship thus becomes unique in that the parent's 'I' breaks free of itself without ceasing to be 'I.' As stated earlier, it is the only relationship in which the self becomes other and, extraordinarily, survives.[74] The 'I' breaks free of what ties it to itself, so that it can reach out to another,

---

[73] This is particularly evident not in rugby players to take a cliché example of supposed virility, but in transgendered persons where the power exerted over a biological given often—but not always—affords little or no weakening.

[74] I follow here Levinas's argument developed in *Time and the Other*. However, as should be self-evident, this reading attempts to rethink his argument anew without loosing sight of its uncompromising, but often forgotten eschatological and transcendental radicality. See Levinas, *Time and the Other*.

even become other to itself and this breaking out is precisely what opens the future: the fact that the 'I' suddenly becomes un-recognizable, transformed nearly beyond recognition.

This process of becoming other to the self-sufficiency of the virile self (or the process of giving space and time to the unrecognizable) therefore opens up the possibility of a beyond all possibilities, an openness to an unpredictable and undeterminable future. In a way, unlike the obsessive self-control of virility, parenting implies a future with another (self) who is necessarily out of control and this even if the child is a model of perfection.

THE QUESTION

What happens then if a schism occurs between virility and parenting? In other words, what happens if the potential for parenting is recurrently left aside and only virility is given pre-eminence? Can the time of ('gay') sexual pleasure truly manage to open another dimension of temporality, irreducible either to the imminence of death or to the future announced by parenting?

The argument sought here is that my erotic encounter with this man is driven neither by desire nor by a mere need (a merely hedonic virile economy typical of the 'gay' scene, for example), but by an opening to a hidden future that manages nonetheless to eschew both parenting and death. In other words, my love for this man opens a dimension that still manages to go beyond being. How is this possible?

CARESS-AS-TOUCH

Caressing or touching[75] this brawny and hairy man is a peculiar act. However much I attempt to please and satisfy

---

[75] In contrast to what was explored in chapter 2, "Sexual Difference," the caress in this context—the context of the difference of sexes—necessarily falls in the realm of the senses. As stated before, Derrida

his appetites, my caress is not 'for him' strictly speaking; but for a future never future enough. In other words and to follow Levinas's vocabulary, the caress does not know what it seeks. Aside from the economy of the orgasm, the caress is also, affectively and effectively, the anticipation of a future without content, an anticipation that opens onto the ungraspable.

To use a different Levinasian vocabulary, I could also say that my erotic encounter expresses a way of being worried by a difference that never ceases to be different. This worry does not drive me (back) in search of a reassuring sameness; it goes instead towards what is more than me or him—an alluring and dangerous 'beyond us.' The caress seeks not a union of two, but on the contrary, a difference that my worry never manages to overcome.

My caress therefore seeks a future that is measured by neither procreation nor death, but by the call to the birth of self and other, that is, to what is not yet human. In other words, when I touch him, I search for what has not yet come into being; my caress seeks what (in or all over me and him) has not yet become (of me and of him).

This relation with the future is therefore *not* exclusively channelled into a power or an empowerment (which would be the inevitable outcome of and return to virility); it invites instead a time that is paradoxically both mine and not-mine; a possibility for myself that is also a possibility for the other.

These are strange kinds of possibilities, because they do not enter into the logical essence of what is usually understood

---

exposes this type of caress in a commentary on Levinas's work: "The caress gives or takes. And/or it gives and takes. In giving it takes; it gives to take; it takes up giving—what one calls pleasure a little hastily. In pleasure, the caress besieges us, it invests us with a non-theoretical and besetting question, with a worry constitutive of pleasure itself: 'What is this pleasure? What is that? Where does it come from? From the other or from me? Am I taking it? Am I giving it? Is it the other who gives it to me? Or takes it form me? The time of this pleasure is it that I am giving it myself?' And so forth. And if these hypotheses were not contradictory or incompatible, how would one need to think them? Declare them? Even confess them?": Jacques Derrida, *On Touching Jean-Luc Nancy*, 75.

by the possible. No ability or capacity can predetermine them. Contingency rules these possibilities, and that is why they make 'us' dangerously prevaricate between the same and the other, the worry and the difference. There would be no caress if this were not the case.

In this way, and contrary to all expectations in this sultry man-on-man scenario, we still bestow life on each other. Our love manages to fecundate both of us in turn. We do not become *re*born; we simply give birth to each other, that is, to an 'other' that neither of us can recognize *properly*. In other words, we love each other as the bodies that we surprisingly become, that is, for their very inhumanity.

Once again, this is not hedonistic or a self-enclosed battle of virilities or willies; this is on the contrary a love that seeks to disjoin space and time and therefore the solid certainty of the virile subject *who always believes himself stronger than space and time.* In other words, this is a love that seeks to dislocate the delusions of mastery, making bodies shiver for being unable, *at last*, to predict and/or project into the future.

EQUALS

The alterity sought here is obviously of a different register than that provided by death or by a child. It concerns a futurity that frets about on the edges of eschatology and messianism; a fretting that re-inscribes a 'between' that is neither masculine nor feminine; a birth that accomplishes not a return to the same, but another (self/other) whose face (in a Levinasian sense) will break in ways that are always utterly unrecognizable.

However, not unlike for death and for a child, this alterity (sought here where the sun never has a chance of shining) still remains undecidable: at once me and the other, at once historical and a-historical. Flesh and bones, this *new* self/other becomes the intangible, but very real resistance—with all its spatial and temporal connotations—against the tide of presence.

In this way, our love, this love devoid of all potential parenting, still manages to open another dimension of temporality. The dried up cum-cloth has obviously no future; it will always already remain locked within the economy of the same, but—however cliché this sounds—our love is here to stay, each time defying what we mean by sur-vival.[76] Is this not precisely this defiance that scares homophobes so much?

The 'outcome' of this resistance against the tide of presence ('I') or this defiance against reproductive futurity, in other words, the 'outcome' of this alternate future to babies or death, creates a strange form of equality between men and women, 'heterosexuals' and 'homosexuals' (or any other invented abstraction): 'we' are all equals as makers of the future; 'we' are the arch-originary carrying forth of self-engendering-the-other, whether 'we' raise children or 'breed' HIV till death do us part. End(s) indeed always meet so that there is future, even if it is short.

In this way, no acquisition of children can open the future more than 'us' not as a couple or collectivity, but as we come together as separation. The child as the 'door' to the future is only an ephemeral illusion because as soon as birth has taken place, the child will also have to negotiate the bounds that finitude imposes on him or her. In defiance (if it is a boy, endlessly disposing the tissue, sock, banana peel, or indeed the cum cloth) or in a determined move or absentmindedness

---

[76] The word 'sur-vival' is here left open because it does not refer to some kind of vitalist survival, but following Derrida, to what lives over and beyond life. As Judith Butler clearly explains: "[Derrida] is clear about the finality of death, but he returns to the task of affirming what he calls survival, *la survie*. He references Walter Benjamin who, in "The Task of the Translator," makes a distinction between *überleben* (survival) of a part, surviving death, as a book can survive the death of its author or a child survives the death of a parent, and *fortleben*, living on, continuing to live, the continuation of life itself. 'Survival' carries these two meanings, continuing to live, but also, he emphasizes, living after death." See Judith Butler, "On Never Having Learned How to Live," *Differences* 16, no. 3 (2005): 30, and Jacques Derrida, "Je suis en guerre contre moi-même," *Le Monde* (18 Aug. 2004).

(putting semen to use), he or she will also remain the very invention of the other.

6. The Factory

INTRODUCTION

Most of time the focus is on the vertical conduit or delivery system that shamelessly always tries to reach up as high as is humanly possible. Any discourse for which this upright conduit is standard emphasizes the triumph of verticality, signification, and self-possession. For some, this conduit is the alpha and omega, the beginning and the end, the (toy-like) entertainment prop that sets the standard for everything else...

But what is one to think of the site of production underneath? Little attention is indeed paid to what we will call here the factory. By over-emphasizing the heroic uprightness of the tubular member, man-folk and their relationships to other bodies, male or female, suffer from an unfair distortion: everything is always about the mastery of the earth and skies, and not about the work that goes on in order for this *supposed* mastery to take place.

But this is not all. By over-emphasizing erectility over what goes on below, the general tendency is to ignore the fact that the factory, contrary to the endlessly repeated selfishness attributed to the vertical conduit (and men by default), produces something 'for another.' This 'product for another' is a difficult one to describe, as it is never neutral: it is both potentially positive and negative, a threat and a gift; the most problematic because emblematic double-bind offering men can put forward.

In this way, and unlike verticality, signification, and self-possession and therefore pleasure, the site of production necessarily implies 'two'; it is, however dangerous it is to recognize this, inescapably social. This does not necessarily emphasize reproduction. Even when no procreation is sought out, the factory still produces 'for the other' even when there is violence—we will come back to this.

Overall, when it comes to that which is below, the hackneyed question is always invariably and tiresomely: is there a factory there or not? This has nothing to do with the visibility of the factory (whether it is hidden or dangling noticeably) or the invisibility of its work. This has to do with the factory's ability or capacity to generate what it takes for the upright character to play its role. As will become evident, this commonplace ur-question refers to something infinitely more complex than at first anticipated.

As the above references to 'tubular member,' 'conduit' and 'upright character' clearly show, the following text will not address the mechanisms, structures, and discourses imposed by that *other* metaphor, the monolithic psychoanalytical ogre known as the phallus. This does not mean to invalidate, evade or discard any link between the body and a whole range of already existing metaphors, symbols, and tools used by that discipline or practice. I simply have no expertise in articulating what follows from a psychoanalytical perspective.

The aim instead is to put forward a different metaphor (i.e. here the factory) in order to address, in one's own terms, the experience of a living male body, even if it is deeply problematic in other disciplines or practices such as psychoanalysis (in a way, what follows is ripe for the couch: a promising narrative full, no doubt, of neurotic symptoms of castration anxieties and the like). However, the idea is, as has been shown many times before, that the phallus is not the only signifier of masculinity and masculine sexuality is not exclusively phallocentric. Something else is also at stake and this is what will remain to be shown with this alternative or complementary metaphor.

Inevitably the danger in elaborating another metaphor of this kind is to be accused of yet another simplistic biological reductionism ('ironically,' alongside that other reduction, the phallus). In order to prevent this danger, I can only reference here Jean-Luc Nancy who says that the body is not just a biological, social or cultural entity; it is also that which first articulates space (and) time. The body, following Jean-Luc Nancy and Merleau-Ponty before him, is indeed that which takes place at the limit; it is an event at the limit of sense, in the emergence of sense and signification. The body does not *have* sense (or have a phallus) and it *is* not sense (be a phallus). The body can only be "the taking place of sense [*l'avoir-lieu du sens*]."[77]

As the taking place of sense, the body can only generate metaphors, symbols and tools (the phallus, the factory, etc.) only if it also exceeds, defies, and challenges them at the same time. This is the body's double bind, one which no disciplines can overcome once and for all, and this however much they try. In a way, the body is precisely that which forces disciplines to always become unrecognizable. *In the end*, the body always wins.

Armed in this way against the accusation of crude biologism, the aim of the following chapter is therefore to think a more provisional, heuristic and personal gesture that goes— on all accounts—with the sense of *this* body, that is, with the way this body exceeds itself. The aim behind this gesture is to suggest the idea of turning the discussion on the male body (and its ontological structure) towards not so much a different metaphor, but a different mode of operation and description.

Finally, please note that the following reference to the factory is deliberately and self-consciously intended to come

---

[77] Nancy, *Corpus*, 119.

across as butch, sturdy, and robust. Considering the fact that this site of production is physically rather fragile, one would have perhaps expected a more delicate or dainty metaphor. But this would have never worked. The aim behind the use of this cliché or macho metaphor is really to emphasize something very common to men: their (obsessive) propensity to produce.

BROMIDE

The factory is a dual-chambered excrescence. It is strategically located between elevation and descent into darkness. The reason for this position appears to be to keep the factory at a low temperature. For this reason, the factory has the curious characteristic of continually contracting or extending itself in order to keep the ambient temperature at optimal productive conditions. This movement up and down is completely involuntary and results in often-amusing changes in appearance.

In each chamber, the factory produces its goods and the substance that gives life to them (as well as wanted or unwanted side effects elsewhere—unusual growths or changes in tone, for example). The factory itself isn't heavy or large, but ludicrously small in comparison to the importance of its role: twenty grams at most and about five centimetres in length.

A common myth, based on some obscure etymological homonymy, says that the factory is the witness to the (in)exhaustible work of the pipe above.[78] In other words, there would be no law without these witnesses guaranteeing the assumed authority of the 'one.' And the fact that it is located in a dual-chambered setting confirms this obscure homonymy, thus attributing to them a certain truth-value: one confirming what they other has 'witnessed.'

There is a whole series of words—some caricatural—that conjures up the factory's attributes. In most cases, these have

---

[78] For such an etymological homonymy, see Joshua T. Katz, "*Testimonia Ritus Italici*: Male Genitalia, Solemn Declarations, and a New Latin Sound Law," *Harvard Studies in Classical Philology* 98 (1998): 183–217.

been made to include the tubular member.[79] If one confines oneself to the site of production these words are: tool-kit, gear, accessory, the machines, the instruments, and even the equipment, to take only examples from the specific 'builder's' vocabulary opted here. The most significant is perhaps 'the attire,' which designates the couple of objects destined to perform the particular task necessary to accomplish the symbolic work of the over-exposed one above.

However, the factory is not always well equipped. Sometimes the accessory is insufficient, the tool-kit malfunctions, the machinery is inefficient, the instruments fail to perform, the gear is unsatisfactory. When this happens, the law of the 'one' becomes debatable and war rages on. But however unhappy it is, one thing is certain: it never ever goes on strike. Even defeated, it produces till the bitter end.

When in good working order, the factory produces its good on a regular basis, some say, on average 10,000 outputs over a life-time. The goods—referred in some contexts as pearl jam— are tiny, but each one contains constituents that rank in the millions. It takes two and a half months from development to maturity. Once it is mature, the goods can travel a 'mighty' 7.5-10 centimeters or 3-4 inches on their own and survive from 30 seconds to 6 days depending on conditions.

---

[79] In a candidly written text, Paul Smith uncovers probably the most under-studied of these expressions: vas as in *vas deferens*. Drawing inspiration from Michèle Montrelay's work and particularly her text "L'Appareillage," he writes: "The characteristic feature of the pre-oedipal in the male imaginary would then be its va(s)cillation. Vas: that which men carry around in the real and which at the same time contains the unsymbolizable; it represents that which we consist in *and* that which we don't symbolize; that which we both carry and lose; or, to use an older vocabulary, that which we both accumulate and spend": Paul Smith "Vas," *Camera Obscura* 6, no. 2 (May 1988): 101. See also Judith Halberstam's commentary in relation to female masculinity in: Judith Halberstam, "The Good, the Bad, and the Ugly: Men, Women, and Masculinity," in *Masculinity Studies and Feminist Theory: New Directions,* ed. Judith Kegan Gardiner (New York: Columbia University Press, 2002), especially 354–6.

Of course, the end result of this work is that once the goods enter the infamous pipe, its goods can travel at a 'whoopee' 28 mph, but by then, the show is no longer the factory's. The law of the 'one' takes over and witnesses change.

FILTH

The process of fabrication and delivery is often seen as a form of defilement. It is a form of filth because it transgresses borders, which means that it also transgresses identities. The reason this is often mentioned is because identities are often tied to their physical borders and anything that passes through these borders is seen as a threat to its supposed self-containment.

Of course, the goods produced in this factory are not unique in being seen as a form of filth that threatens stability and autonomy. Others, some of which cannot be mentioned here, have the same worrisome and dangerous status.

However, something distinguishes it from these other threats. Julia Kristeva indeed says that the factory's produce is simply more abject than others.[80] It is abject because, once it is out, it still stands for the possibility of life and as such, it is still, as mentioned earlier, out of control, accidental, chancy. This is more controversial than it seems at first because the goods are effectively the only type of filth that potentially remains outside of all forms of mastery.

Outside of any form of control, the goods fall outside of the law. No one can indeed explain or regulate rationally why one of its constituents is chosen over all others. Why this repro-duction rather than another and why this one rather than nothing? The law of the 'one' never rests on certainty, but on the dicey play of a multiplicity run amok.

All this comes to ask the more hackneyed question, why life rather than death? No law will be able to extend its jurisdiction

---

[80] See Julia Kristeva, *Powers of Horror: An Essay on Abjection,* trans. L.S. Roudiez (New York: Columbia University Press, 1982), 43–5.

over such a mystery. A cast of the dice never indeed abolishes chance, as the old Mallarmé would say.

It might therefore be filth and abject, but the factory's output has a curious propensity to remind human beings—men and women—that ultimately no one has control over life, not even its proud or shamefaced producers and the ones who accept it carelessly, suffer it in disgust, or embrace it productively.

COGLIONE

This perhaps explains why, unlike the pole, the factory is often seen as an object of ridicule. Some people are embarrassed by it, fearing perhaps that the factory is a far too laughable a symbol for man-folk's inability to master life. Other people even refuse to touch it, fearing perhaps that, whether they want it or not, they might be part of the ridicule.

As an 'object' of ridicule, the factory is often therefore compared to something idiotic or stupid. So much so that there are some people who love to kick, knee, squeeze, or otherwise abuse the factory. When struck, the factory causes extreme pain, which can be either welcome or not.

But this isn't all; in addition to being compared with something stupid, the factory is also considered by many as an ugly appendage. The fact that its two chambers are most often asymmetrically positioned could have something to do with it. Asymmetry never figures as a criterion for beauty in aesthetic treaties, the number of fig or maple leaves and loincloths in the history of art partly attest to this.

Finally, the factory is also used as an expression of contempt, annoyance, or defiance, clearly indicating that these dangly oblong spheres are really of no importance, that what counts is the singularity and mastery of that which is above. In these cases, other terms are usually used—often by cocky and obstreperous people.

In any case, what all these unpleasant references suggest is that the factory is there to remind us that there is always something a bit risible about man-folk. As Diderot rightly remarked, there is always a bit of testicle at the bottom of men's most sublime feelings and their purest tenderness.[81] Some of men's most awe-inspiring and most hideous thoughts, creations, and ideologies would perhaps never have seen the light of day if they hadn't been driven by the annoyingly tiresome work of these odd oblong spheres.

EXTRAVAGANCE

Notwithstanding its ridiculousness, ugliness, and comical aspects, the factory has a curious, but not unique characteristic that distinguishes it from all other factories. Its machinery constantly produces at a loss. The factory participates, to follow a specific Bataillean vocabulary, in what could be termed forms of non-productive expenditures.[82]

This curious characteristic unintentionally challenges the commonly held belief (held by both Capitalism and Communism, for example) in the primacy of exchange as the sphere of meaning and production. The factory indeed produces at a ridiculous loss because out of an average 10,000 outputs in a sixty-year life span, only a truly ridiculous number is productive.

This clearly shows that, overall, the factory is the unruly reverse of work, utility, politics, laws, truth, or knowledge and therefore pleasure. As such, the factory is really the opposite of what is usually understood by economy; it is, like Adam's parting rib, that which is precisely without return, what is always in excess of conventional economy, thus contradicting

---

[81] Denis Diderot, "Lettre à Damilaville, 3 novembre 1760," in *Correspondance*, Vol. III (novembre 1759 - décembre 1761), ed. Georges Roth (Paris: Minuit, 1957), 120.

[82] The following argument is borrowed from Georges Bataille's analysis of eroticism. The focus of this chapter is intended to push Bataille's idea in another direction in order to emphasize the liminality of the male body's erotic afterlife. See Georges Bataille, *The Accursed Share*, Vol. 1, trans. R. Hurley (Cambridge: MIT Press, 1991).

or compensating for man's obsession with productivity, effectiveness, leadership, order, authenticity, and wisdom.

In this way, not unlike laughter or drunkenness, this factory operates paradoxically in a non-fatherly way, some might even say in a perpetually adolescent manner: it operates on the basis of an economy that is pure destruction, a repetitive squandering of a by-product of health or ill health and this, whether in a lovely 'heterosexual' or hard-core bare-backing environment.

In a way and if one is permitted to make ruthless appropriations, death and life on earth are not due to the benevolence of God or a system that can be scientifically comprehended; it is *partly* the result of a senseless and wasteful squandering of energy. In other words, death and life are not due to a thought-out plan, but to the fortuitous outcome of a preposterous extravagance.

Now it would be wrong to understand this extravagance as something that can be quantified or qualified, calculated or analysed. However much references are made here to specific number of 'outputs,' the extravagance remains always already un-representable because it lies outside of any form of totalisation. The same goes with artistic experiments (Duchamp's *Faulty Landscape* 1946, for example): they can never *properly* represent this extravagance.

The activity of squandering recklessly, which curiously and in all modesty, goes on a par, as Bataille would say, with the sun's endless prodigality, knows indeed no transcription. This does not mean that it can only be embodied: pure somatic experience, for example. This simply means that the anarchy of its flow can never be translated, classified, ordered. In other words, unlike the phallus, which always equals 'one,' the factory's produce is alien to any economic system that would reduce it in order to allow it to finally signify as this or that.

Of course, one could argue that once the goods are channelled through utility, they are necessarily—and perhaps now more than ever—always already *a* form of commodity. The factory does not obviously operate out of pure generosity. It patently operates within a utility framework, that is, through an economic system, or as part of a set of contractual agreements (whether solitary, with another, or with others). In this way, what is essentially pure loss is nonetheless still channelled through profit.

But, however much extravagance is used for selfish gratification and turned into a product for sale (from prostitution, to bukkake orgies, to fertility clinics), the factory itself remains always already a work of prodigality that only an unfortunate accident, a severe localised illness, or death can stop. The factory is one of the few things in life that produces life, most of which is murdered, thus paradoxically emphasizing the impossibility of distinguishing it from death. Mother nature has obviously no regard for human ethics or feelings because it clearly never ceases to prevaricate between life and death.

UNRLY GIFT

There is one major consequence to this reckless extravagance that is dangerous to express, for it concerns, as announced in the introduction to this chapter, its destination, which, as we will see, is not a destiny: 'for the other.'

However problematic it is to acknowledge the following, the fact remains that this 'for the other' is really (also) a call out of self ('self' understood here not as *idem*, but as *ipseity*, that is, as what is already produced and inscribed as an unstable arrangement of sex and gender). This is indeed a tricky issue because the focus on the conduit above usually determines the whole machinery (and by reductive extension, men in general) as exclusively self-centered and selfish, and therefore as necessarily violent.

The argument here is the fact that to produce in such prodigal fashion implies an exteriorization that contradicts the conduit's violent unsociableness. The factory's work is a call out of self because it knows no interiority. Giving, whether out of choice or not, is effectively—however infuriating this is—its only possible mode of operation. This gift is not, as we have seen, an exchange in a conventional economic sense; it is an 'unproductive expenditure' for the other that, beyond selfish pleasure, can know no return.

In order to make sense of this dangerous thought, it is necessary to think the moment this factory is put to use in the encounter with the other—albeit with the same caveat as that announced in the Introduction. When it is put to use, it is so only with the other *as the unforeseeable*. Once again, this does not reduce the other to a state of invisibility or irrelevance. The unforeseeable does not mean absence. She, he, or it is what cannot be projected upon or predicted as self-evident.

In this way, this other is not another person (man or woman), another time (a child), death as such, or a day after history strictly speaking (God). It is whoever or whatever is present at the heart of a shared experience. Present *not only* as a 'total' presence (and thus able to respond in disgust or anticipation) *but also* as trace, the trace of the other—that is, as what or who is not yet.

As such, the factory works—before all articles of faith and philosophy and before all political protest—as a call out of self because it is essentially eschatological at its origin and in each of its aspects. In other words, the factory is one of the few 'things' that is able to produce some 'thing' that crosses over to the other and still manages to remain potentially a 'beyond death' (and this even if it is temporarily mediated by the gaze).

The fact of being potentially 'beyond death' is what distinguishes it from any other gesture (love, for example) because, as we have seen in the previous chapter, it is the only opening onto the future that exceeds all future-presents, that is, all forms of projection or predictions. As Levinas rightly observes against Heidegger and conventional readings of *The Song of Songs*, it is *Eros* and not love that is stronger than death.[83]

This obviously does not mean that, because it is intimately coupled with pleasure, it is not *also* irascibly violent, inescapably self-centred, and unbearably selfish. 'Take that' or 'you want it?' are the usual expressions used in pornography

---

[83] Levinas, *Time and the Other*, 76.

to express such an unbearable violence. However, amidst all this brutality, this also expresses a call-out-of-self that paradoxically reaches out to what is no longer *ipse* (and this, even if celibacy, chastity, and abstinence are the chosen options).

This also does not imply the stability of a possession, the security of an always-replenished gift 'shop,' or the assurance that life is secure because of man's endless propensity to produce. Instability, unreliability, and contingency rule this productivity. If this was not the case, then men would be permanently 'turned'-on working fountains: a parody of life's munificence (cf. Bruce Nauman's *Self-Portrait as Fountain*, 1966–7).

However, notwithstanding this contingency (or perhaps because of it), there is a rather repetitive emphasis that perhaps should be taken in consideration: not everything is self-absorbed, self-seeking, self-serving and this, however much the act itself is inescapably wrapped up in the constitution of self (*ipseity*). In other words, however debilitating and dangerously unpredictable horniness can be, it is also paradoxically, a way of rejecting the overwhelming self-sufficiency of virility (as defined in chapter 5, "End(s) Meet").[84]

In this way, and however unsettling or disturbing this is if one considers humanity's long history of virile violence, the factory's work is a self-serving appeal to be freed from self (*ipseity*). In other words, the factory's tireless work is perhaps the most unsettling of men's call, for it remains secretly a selfish plea to no longer be selfish—a plea that can perhaps be translated each time anew as: 'bollocks to Being.' A rather

---

[84] In saying this, I deliberately remain prior to the constitution of the subject as phallus—hence my repeated reference to *ipseity* as an unstable arrangement (in lieu of *idem* as a recollected identity). As such, I slightly differ from Michèle Montrelay's idea that ejaculation is a loss of subjectivity in relation to the phallus. For Montrelay's ideas, see: Michèle Montrelay, "L'Appareillage," *Cahiers Confrontations* 6 (Spring 1982): 33–43. For commentaries, see Smith, "Vas," 95–100; and Murat Aydemir, *Images of Bliss: Ejaculation, Masculinity, Meaning* (Minneapolis: University of Minnesota Press, 2007), 118–9.

disconcerting thought when considering the overwhelming presence of the money shot in pornography.

7. Couplings

INTRODUCTION

—Woman was set apart from man, but she came after him.[85]

—Or woman is above man, but comes after him.

---

[85] This first sentence is Annette Aranowicz's translation of a sentence by Emmanuel Levinas taken from *Nine Talmudic Readings* (Bloomington: Indiana University Press, 1990), 173. Levinas's original sentence—first read out at a colloquium entitled "Ish and Isha or the Other par excellence" in Paris in 1971 —reads: "La femme a été prélevée sur l'homme, mais est venue après lui": Emmanuel Levinas, *L'Autre dans la conscience Juive* (Paris: Presses Universitaires de France, 1973), 121. There is no space here to propose an alternative translation (for example: "Woman was extracted from man, but came after him" or "woman was made before man, but came after him"). The choice of translation is made here in order to emphasize the importance of chronology in Levinas's choice of words. For a further commentary (and yet another translation of this sentence), see: Jacques Derrida, "At This Very Moment in This Work, Here I Am," in *Re-Reading Levinas*, ed. Robert Bernasconi and Simon Critchley (London: The Athlone Press, 1991), 40.

This very short exchange of opinions provides two different ways one can conceive the relation between man and woman as two opposed genders, that is, as two bio-anthropological beings confined to the logic of the difference of sexes. These two different ways are not unique. Others could have been envisaged.

In this particular exchange, the first sentence epitomizes the classic Biblical narrative, one that emphasizes a chronological progression: Eve was created (or set apart) from Adam's rib, side, face, or tail and was therefore secondary in the history of creation. By repeating the story twice (and lessening in the process the role of the conjunction 'but'), the first sentence therefore accentuates a teleological order of priority: first man, then woman.

The second attempts to think woman not as derived from man, as the common readings of the Bible wants us to believe, but, as the use of the present tense and the glaring impropriety of the conjunction 'but' intimates, as part of a game in which no order of priority is determined in advance. This second sentence will form the focus of this final chapter.

The aim behind this second sentence and therefore behind this reconfiguration or, more precisely, this temporal rephrasing of the old Biblical narrative is two-fold:

Firstly, to show that—paradoxically, considering the chosen sentence—it is no longer possible to claim equality between man and woman as two opposed autonomous entities.[86] As we have already seen, equality always returns us to the same

---

[86] I am obviously aware that this is not a new argument. For example, Elizabeth Grosz rightly sums up Irigaray's views on this topic: "Any egalitarian project, whether directed to the equalization of relations between the sexes, or between races, classes or ethnicities, is, for Irigaray, antagonistic to the project of specification of differences. Egalitarian projects entail a neutral measure for the attainment of equality, a measure that invariably reflects the value of the dominant position": Elizabeth Grosz, "The Nature of Sexual Difference," *Angelaki: Journal of the Theoretical Humanities* 17, no. 2 (2012): 73. My aim in repeating this argument is to draw attention to how a question of temporality exposes the strict impossibility of equality and this, way before any political (egalitarian) project has been formulated.

and therefore to man. The study of this second sentence will attempt—and attempt only—to demonstrate how to avoid this seemingly inevitable return.

Secondly, to show, once again, but this time, from a different perspective, that it is no longer possible to think of mankind on the basis of a singular origin: first, God, then androgynous/male Adam, and then Eve. As we have seen, man and woman are born together as separation (cf. chapter 4, "The Side Story"). Their 'dislocation' or 'disjointedness' shows that *when it comes to their* (measured) *spatial and temporal interaction*, they always find themselves at least in the text— and this is what remains to be shown—both paradoxically in a symmetrical and asymmetrical relation.

Please note that the following text will remain purely exegetical,[87] i.e. it will only attempt to be a commentary on the second sentence above. As such, it will not attempt to rethink the Biblical narrative or to put forward an analysis of how man and woman (should) relate to each other in 'real' life. If such exegetical analysis influences positively the way the Bible is read or the way man and woman relate to each other, then there will be an assumption that this is a good thing.

Although the following stays at an exegetical level, there will be here no specific theological reading or analysis of the

---

[87] I am aware of the dangers that exist in remaining at a purely exegetical level. The intention here is not to reduce woman to a mere abstract referent and ignore the historically and geo-politically disenfranchised. Like all words, woman or man can no longer be understood at a unifying essentialist level, but (at least) as a doubling of levels: an onto-epistemological and a historical bio-anthropological. As this book attempts to show, these levels cannot be understood independently of each other. And as this paragraph shows, the hope here is therefore to re-think once again (and by me here, inevitably and once again, fraudulently) the relation between man and woman at an exegetical level in the hope that 'subsequently' the *word* 'woman' no longer simply stands for what Spivak calls the 'gendered subaltern.' Gayatri Chakravorty Spivak, "Feminism and Deconstruction, Again: Negotiating with Unacknowledged Masculinism," in *Between Feminism and Psychoanalysis*, ed. Teresa Brennan (London: Routledge, 1993), 220.

passages in The Bible that refer to the theme of this sentence. Many scholars have examined the discrepancy between Adam and Eve. From Jonathan ben Uzziel to Rashi and from Rabbi Samson Raphael Hirsch to Azila Talit Reisenberger, the list is long and to pretend adding something new to this long list would simply be preposterous in the present context. The following chapter is simply inspired by the work of two scholars: Levinas's Talmudic Readings and Derrida's careful reading of Levinas, notably in his very much un-examined text, "At This Very Moment in This Work, Here I Am." Once again, there will be no masterly commentary on these scholar's work[88]; only a side reading with the intention of departing elsewhere.

QUESTIONS

Woman is above man, but comes after him. This curious sentence raises at least three crucial sets of questions:

Firstly, is it at all possible to say something so irretrievably odd: at once gracious and bad mannered: woman higher than man, but also left behind? What kind of political correctness is this?

Secondly, is it really possible to divide genders in this way: between a space extending upwards ('above') at the end of which woman 'is' and a time ('after') allowing man to 'be'? Do genders need to be spaced and temporized in this way?

And finally, if one were to follow the logic of such juxtaposition, why choose the prepositions 'above' and 'after' instead of 'below' and 'before'? In other words, can one write: 'man is below woman, but comes before her' and if yes, does this alter the meaning of what is at stake here?

---

[88] The list of commentators who have engaged in cross-readings of Levinas and Derrida is extensive and cannot be replicated here. I can only report readers to the careful work of Richard A. Cohen, Hent de Vries, Martin Hägglund, John Llwelyn, Jill Robins, Martin C. Srajek, Chloe Taylor and Agata Zielinski amongst others.

These questions will be addressed in the following text, but in a non-sequential way.

LOFTY-LOWLY/LATE-EARLY

This sentence is intended to refer to an inextricable perpendicular relation: a vertical order (above-below) intercepting a horizontal order (before-after). It is a relation and not a dislocation or disjointedness as in chapter 2, because we are here in the realm of the difference of sexes and therefore in *measured* space and time. In such context, genders relate to one another; they express narratives about each other and these narratives, whether 'straight' or 'queer,' take space and time to unfold.

The aim of this specific perpendicular relation is to avoid thinking subjectivity (man or woman) outside of an inter-subjective structure. Subjectivity is always already structured by the other not in a relation of equality (man recognizing his equal or his opposite in woman, for example) or inequality (man and woman relating to each other as god or monster, divine or diabolical), but in a perpendicular relation that, as we will see, is both equal *and* unequal.

How can one make sense of this perpendicular *relation*?

The sentence in question here involves a man and a woman, who on all accounts could be alter egos to each other. The fact that one is above and comes after does not necessarily preclude the fact that one order can indeed be equal to the other. Man and woman remain in this sentence overall equals.

However, if one takes their respective positions in consideration, one could also make the following two statements: firstly, woman is always loftier in relation to man who is always lowly. Secondly, one could also say that man is always early in relation to woman who is always late.

The question that ensues here is therefore this: how does her lateness relate with her loftiness? Alternatively, the question is also this: how does his earliness relate with the fact of being lowly?

These questions cannot be answered simply because it is not possible to decide between loftiness and lowliness *and* between lateness and earliness. This impossibility to decide is firstly due to the fact that there cannot be a single vantage point (male, female, neutral) from which to relate these terms together. Without exterior and therefore without the possibility of objectification, the vantage point simply does not exist.

This impossibility to decide is also due to the inevitable substitutability of the relation (cf. "Sexual Difference"): Woman does not exclusively express a spatial coordinate (above / below) and man does not exclusively express a temporal one (before / after). Both *create* and *take* space and time while 'being' (in) space and time as such.

Their relation is therefore one of vicissitude: he appears in this sentence lowly and too early, but he could also equally be, who knows, lofty and too late. The orders could be substituted and this substitutability coupled with this lack of vantage point are effectively what prevents anyone from relating loftiness with lateness, earliness with lowliness.

In this way, it is impossible to ascribe a one-to-one correspondence between man and woman as if each would hold a neat parcel of space *and* time. In a perpendicular relation of vicissitude, man and woman trouble each other as they trouble space and time, thus making it impossible to conceive a strict equality between them—at least not in a conventional understanding of equality.

The troubled structure in question here is therefore an odd perpendicular relation of vicissitude between man and woman that cannot be detached from the way space and time relate to each other: spacing (and) temporizing space and time. (Once again, this perpendicularity is neither unique nor is it a universal structure. If the argument above has any validity, it needs to assume that other 'relation' would be equally true.)

DIACHRONY

In order to articulate further such a relation, it is crucial to remember (cf. Sexual Difference) that this relation operates effectively under a specific law: the law of absolute heteronomy (diachrony). This law establishes that the relation between man and woman is always already a relation of vicissitude that is *also* incalculable and unpredictable.

In other words, man and woman relate to each other and this relation of vicissitude is always already in the hands of contingency or the unforeseeable. There is no other way of understanding this relation. If there were another way of doing so, one would automatically return to an understanding of subjectivity (man or woman) as self-contained objects *in* space *and* time.

However, once again, this law does not imply that there is something external (God, for example) that simply renders genders prone to contingency. No God rules the law of absolute heteronomy; it is always already in the hands of those who create, make, and take space and time, that is, it is always already in the hands of man, woman and their own (un)predictability.

This relation between genders can never therefore be autonomous strictly speaking, that is, synchronized as some logically recognizable 'thing.' In order for it to *also* be incalculable and unpredictable, in order for it to *also* be absolute, it cannot be turned into 'a moment' in space and time. The law would no longer be effective. Man and woman would obey a different law—a homonymous law, for example—where nothing could tell them apart and space and time would have no meaning whatsoever.

The law of absolute heteronomy that puts man and woman always already in a perpendicular relation effectively comes with their own diachrony; i.e. it is what (il)logically relates space and time and therefore genders together. It is (il)logical because, as we will see, it both makes sense *and* fails to make sense. For obvious reasons, diachrony or the law of absolute heteronomy can never entirely make sense.

But in that case, can one really say this?

THE PHRASE

The chosen sentence aims to match the unruly operational principle it describes. This is done with the use of a specific tense: the present tense indeed refuses *here* a teleological order of priority, thus equalizing—albeit here oddly—man and woman. There are here together in the present and they understand each other with the use of a synchronic tense.

But this is not quite exact, the sentence also manages to disrupt its own synchronic grammar: the sentence, like the relation it describes, somewhat (also) fails to make sense (the 'but' is effectively given here all its weight, thus rendering the sentence illogical) and yet still makes sense (the sentence remains indeed grammatically correct).

As such, the sentence is representative of the relation between man and woman: it demonstrates the fact that the relation of vicissitude between man and woman is a logical absurdity[89]: that on the one hand, it is symmetrical, it somewhat makes sense, it is outwardly logical, and on the other,

---

[89] I borrow this expression from Jacques Derrida and develop it at length in *After 'Rwanda.'* Commenting on Levinas's work, Derrida writes: "The other as alter ego signifies the other as other, irreducible to my ego, precisely because it is an ego, because it has the form of the ego. The egoity of the other permits him to say 'ego' as I do; and this is why he is Other and not a stone, or a being without speech in my real economy. This is why, if you will, he is face, can speak to me, understand me, and eventually command me. Dissymmetry itself would be impossible without this symmetry, which is not of the world, and which, having no real aspect, imposes no limit upon alterity and dissymmetry—makes them possible, on the contrary. This dissymmetry is an economy in a new sense; a sense which would probably be intolerable to Levinas. Despite the *logical absurdity* of this formulation, this economy is the transcendental symmetry of two empirical asymmetries": Derrida, "Violence and Metaphysics," 157, my emphasis.

it is radically dissymmetrical, it fails to make sense or, more precisely, it falls out of sense, it is absurd, not in the sense of foolishness, but in the sense of what knows no logical ground.

In this way, both the sentence and, speculatively, the reality to which it refers, manage to weave together what is out of synch and out of grammar (diachrony) with what is recognizable as being in synch and in grammar (synchrony). However, because we are in a relation of vicissitude, what is out of synch can also 'be' what is synchronized. In other words, diachrony can also 'be' synchrony and vice-versa. The phrase (and perhaps the reality) can only remain a logical absurdity.

Obviously, and as previously stated, the aim behind this odd sentence and structure is to refuse to be ossified in any one spatial, temporal, social, cultural, or biological construct. For every new space and time, there is a new man or woman and vice-versa. For every new sentence, there is another one, thus keeping the logical absurdity always on edge.

CONTRITION

But the question persists: the above explanation still retains as its essential directive a certain sense: it synchronizes its various elements in order to articulate a relationship between man and woman that is neither oppositional nor hierarchical (and therefore equal or unequal), but both diachronic and synchronic, logical, absurd. In other words, the above explanation still manages to synchronize an onto-epistemological situation, a synchronization that ultimately betrays the law of absolute heteronomy.

The question is therefore this: If one attempts to think exegetically the relation between man and woman, is one then *perpetually* confined to the phallo-logo-centric violence of synchronic (philosophical) grammar—and therefore to the primacy of man? In other words, is this interpretation basically a man's point of view?

For example, as a man and as the 'author' of this text, am I violently appropriating woman by placing her above me while I, obviously, come first? However much I emphasize our vicissitude, am I not being here disingenuous? And if yes, am I then continuing the tradition started by Plato of an understanding of philosophy as an exclusively andro-social—i.e. homo-social—dialogical discourse?

If answers to the above questions are all in the affirmative, am I then yet another cliché in the long history of philosophy? Am I here buggering feminist discourses? Is this temporal recasting of the Biblical narrative a man-on-man immaculate conception based on a random list of texts mostly written by men (from Yahweh to Meillassoux, for example): yet another monstrous offspring?

If all this were indeed the case, then this text would recast itself within the conventional demarcations of gender. It would not understand man and woman as a complex and ambivalent perpendicular relation of signification *and* excess. If this were really the case, then philosophy would have to admit defeat and remain deaf to the spacing (and) temporizing of genders.

So… can this new reconfiguration or rephrasing tells us something we don't already know?

FREEDOM

Perhaps most simply that it is impossible to evade the gendered structure that animates any text or scene whatsoever: diachrony weaving (itself in) synchrony as it pulls apart. In this way, whatever we do and however we read, we can always hear genders resonate, not in perfect harmony (a delusional perfect equality) or absolute disharmony (the total exploitation of the one over the other), but in the anarchy of diachrony, the lawlessness of the law of absolute heteronomy.

The crucial step here is that this impossibility of evading the law of heteronomy does not mean that man and woman or the phrase itself (always) take place in pure randomness. The relation of vicissitude between man and woman can only be always already *amortized*,[90] that is, translated by a synchronic grammar and/or phrased by a philosophy aware of its imminent disaster.

In other words, in order for the perpendicular play between man and woman to be heard properly, the play needs to be amortized (i.e. rendered finite, *ad + mortem*) by a synchronic (i.e. phallo-logo-centric) grammar. There would be no text (and therefore no sex between men and/or women) otherwise.

This does not mean that there is no hope or that yet again the masculine and therefore men in general secretly win the trophy of meaning. If one takes on board both the perpendicular *dislocation* of sexual difference and the perpendicular *relation* of the difference of sexes, then, however much both of these 'structures' are amortized by a synchronic grammar, the conclusion is self-evident: no one wins anything because there is nothing to win: diachrony will never overtake synchrony and vice versa.

This also does not mean that the perpendicular relation envisaged here is effectively unworkable or useless. Although this new reconfiguration or rephrasing is still outside of the political realm (for being mainly exegetical), it still attempts nonetheless to recast the problem differently so as *not* to allow a return to/of the same and to/of the inevitable horror that comes with the gleeful 'assurance' of mastery.

Indeed, with this reconfiguration that neither privileges perfect equality nor aspires to return to a supposedly natural or religious hierarchy, a next step is *perhaps* made here to ensure that women are no longer understood as secondary, forced to 'mime' phallic authority, put on a 'masquerade' or, worse still, attempt a problematic mystical a-logical writing. Synchronic grammar woven in diachrony belongs to all. Monstrous offspring are unavoidable, even in the most radical of feminist philosophies.

---

[90] "Concepts suppose an anticipation, a horizon within which alterity is *amortized* as soon as it is announced precisely because it has let oneself be foreseen. [*Le concept suppose une anticipation, un horizon où l'alterité s'armortit en s'annonçant, et de se laisser prévoir*]": Derrida, 'Violence and Metaphysics,' 118, my emphasis.

With this new reconfiguration or rephrasing, diachrony and women and synchrony and men *and vice versa* can no longer be understood independently of each other, but as part and forming a logical absurdity in which the radically heteronymous is given its say. In this way, man and woman have no other choice but to remain for ever unequal and yet tied to each other in perfect equality because always already creating, making, and taking space and time.

There is no freedom from this logical absurdity because it is the condition of freedom itself. Philosophy must now begin to assume its spacing (and) temporizing genders and to philosophize otherwise in order to respect the exigency that thinking accords with our bodies.

Bibliography

1. PRIMARY SOURCES:

1.1. Emmanuel Levinas

Levinas, Emmanuel. 1969. *Totality and Infinity: An Essay on Exteriority* [1961]. Trans. A. Lingis. Pittsburgh: Duquesne University Press.

—. 1973. *L'Autre dans la conscience Juive*. Paris: Presses Universitaires de France.

—. 1981. *Otherwise than Being or Beyond Essence* [1978]. Trans. A. Lingis. Pittsburgh: Duquesne University Press.

—. 1985. *Ethics and Infinity, Conversations with Philippe Nemo* [1984]. Trans. R.A. Cohen. Pittsburgh: Duquesne University Press.

—. 1987. *Time and the Other* [1979]. Trans. R.A. Cohen. Pittsburgh: Duquesne University Press.

—. 1987. *Collected Philosophical Papers*. Trans. A. Lingis. Dordrecht: Martinus Nijhoff.

—. 1990. *Nine Talmudic Readings* [1968-1977]. Trans. A. Aronowicz. Bloomington: Indiana University Press.

—. 1990. *Difficult Freedom: Essays on Judaism* [1963-1977]. Trans. S. Hand. Baltimore: John Hopkins University Press.

—. 1994. *The Time of the Nations* [1988]. Trans. M.B. Smith. London: The Athlone Press.

—. 1996. *Basic Philosophical Writings*. Ed. Adriaan T. Peperzak, Simon Critchley, and Robert Bernasconi. Bloomington: Indiana University Press.

—. 1996. *Proper Names* [1975]. Trans. M.B. Smith. Stanford: Stanford University Press.

1.2. Jacques Derrida

Derrida, Jacques. 1979. *Speech and Phenomena* [1967]. Trans. D.B. Allison. Evanston: Northwestern University Press.

—. 1980. "The Law of Genre," trans. A. Ronell. *Critical Inquiry* 7, no. 1 (Autumn): 55–81.

—. 1980. "En ce moment même dans cet ourvrage me voice." In *Textes pour Emmanuel Levinas,* ed. François Laruelle, 21–60. Paris: J.-M. Place.

—. 1982. "Choreographies," *Diacritics* 12 (Summer): 66–7.

—. 1982. *Margins of Philosophy*. Trans. A. Bass. Chicago: University of Chicago.

—. 1983. "*Geschlecht*: Sexual Difference, Ontological Difference." *Research in Phenomenology* 13 no. 1: 65–83.

—. 1984. "Voices II." *Boundary* 2, no. 2 (Winter): 79–93.

—. 1984. "Women in the Beehive." *differences: A Journal of Feminist Cultural Studies* 16, no. 3 (Spring): 139–57.

—. 1986. *Glas* [1974]. Trans. J.P. Leavey, Jr. and R. Rand. Lincoln: University of Nebraska Press.

—. 1987. *The Post Card: From Socrates to Freud and Beyond* [1980]. Trans. A. Bass. Chicago: University of Chicago Press.

—. 1991. "At This Very Moment in This Work, Here I Am" [1980], trans. R. Berezdivin. In *Re-Reading Levinas*, ed. Robert Bernasconi and Simon Critchley, 11–47. London: Athlone Press.

—. 1997. "Fourmis: Lectures de la différence sexuelle," trans. E. Prenowitz. In *Rootprints: Memory and Life Writing*, ed. Hélène Cixous and Mireille Calle-Gruber, 119–27. London: Routledge.

—. 2001. "Violence and Metaphysics: An Essay on the Thought of Emmanuel Levinas," trans. A. Bass. In *Writing and Difference* [1967]. London: Routledge.

—. 2002. "The Animal That Therefore I Am [More to Follow]," trans. D. Wills, *Critical Inquiry* 28, no. 2: 369–418.

—. 2005. *On Touching Jean-Luc Nancy*. Trans. C. Irizarry. Stanford: Stanford University Press.

—. 2006. "Scènes des différences: Où la philosophie et la poétique indissociables, font évènement d'écriture." *Littérature* 142 (June): 16–29.

1.3. Jean-Luc Nancy

Nancy, Jean-Luc. 1993. *The Birth to Presence*. Trans. B. Holmes & alia. Stanford: Stanford University Press.

—. 1996. *La Naissance des Seins*. Valence: École régionale des beaux-arts.

—. 2000. *Being Singular Plural*. Trans. R.D. Richardson and A.E. O'Bryne. Stanford: Stanford University Press.

—. 2001. *La pensée dérobée*. Paris: Galilée.

—. 2001. *L'"il y a" du rapport sexuel*. Paris: Galilée.

—. 2003. *A Finite Thinking*. Ed. Simon Spark. Trans. J. Gilbert-Walsh & alia. Stanford: Stanford University Press.

—. 2004. *58 Indices sur le corps et Extension de l'âme*. Quebec: Nota Bene.

—. 2006. "Et après." *Littérature* 2, no. 142 (June): 30–40; doi: 10.3917/litt.142.

—. 2008. *Corpus*. Trans. R.A. Rand. New York: Fordham University Press.

—. 2009. *The Fall of Sleep*. Trans. C. Mandell. New York: Fordham University Press.

Nancy, Jean-Luc & Federico Ferrari. 2002. *Nus sommes (La peau des images)*. Brussels: Yves Gevaert.

2. SECONDARY SOURCES

Introduction

Aurobindo, Sri. 1990. *The Life Divine* [1914-19]. Pondicherry: Sri Aurobindo Ashram Press.

Barber, Stephen M. and David L. Clark. 2002. "Queer Moments: The Performative Temporalities of Eve Kosofsky Sedgwick." In *Regarding Sedgwick: Essays on Queer Culture and Critical Theory*, ed. Stephen M. Barber and David L. Clark, 1–53. London: Routledge.

Benjamin, Walter. 1973. "Theses in the Philosophy of History," trans. H. Zorn. In *Illuminations*, ed. H. Arendt, 245–6. London: Pimlico.

Berger, Anne-Emmanuelle. 2005. "Sexing Différance." In *differences: A Journal of Feminist Cultural Studies* 16, no. 3: 52–67.

Burger, Glenn and Steven F. Kruger. 2001. "Introduction." In *Queering the Middle Ages,* ed. Glenn Burger and Steven F. Kruger, xi–xxii. Minneapolis: University of Minnesota Press.

Dinshaw, Carolyn. 2007. "Temporalities." In *Middle English,* ed. Paul Strohm, 107–23. Oxford: Oxford University Press.

Faludi, Susan. 2000. *Stiffed: The Betrayal of the American Man.* New York: Harper Perennial.

Freeman, Elizabeth, ed. 2007. Special Issue: "Queer Temporalities." *GLQ: A Journal of Lesbian and Gay Studies* 13, no. 2-3; doi: 10.1215/10642684-2006-029.

—. 2010. *Time Binds: Queer Temporalities, Queer Histories.* Durham: Duke University Press.

Halberstam, Judith. 2005. *In a Queer Time and Place: Transgender Bodies, Subcultural Lives.* New York: New York University Press.

Halley, Janet and Andrew Parker eds. 2011. *After Sex? On Writing Since Queer Theory.* Durham: Duke University Press.

Halberstam Judith and Ira Livingston. 1995. "Introduction: Posthuman Bodies." In *Posthuman Bodies,* ed. Judith Halberstam and Ira Livingston, 1–20. Bloomington: Indiana University Press.

Halperin, David. 1995. *Saint Foucault: Towards a Gay Hagiography.* Oxford: Oxford University Press.

Heidegger, Martin. 1992. *The Concept of Time* [1989]. Trans. W. McNeill. London: Blackwell.

Kemp, Jonathan. 2009. "Queer Past, Queer Present, Queer Future." *Graduate Journal of Social Science* 6, Special Issue 1: 3–23.

McCallum, E.L. and Mikko Tuhkanen, eds. 2011. *Queer Times, Queer Becomings.* Albany: State University of New York Press.

Menon, Madhavi. 2005. "Spurning Teleology in Venus and Adonis." *GLQ: A Journal of Lesbian and Gay Studies* 11, no. 4: 491–519.

Martinon, Jean-Paul. 2007. *On Futurity: Malabou, Nancy, and Derrida.* London: Palgrave.

Nietzsche, Friedrich. 1985. *Thus Spoke Zarathustra.* Trans. R.J. Hollingdale. London: Penguin.

O'Rourke, Michael. 2006. "The Roguish Future of Queer Theory." *SQS: Journal of Queer Studies in Finland* 2: 22–47.

—. 2011. "The Afterlives of Queer Theory." *continent.* 1, no. 2: 102–16.

Puar, Jasbir K. 2005. "Queer Times, Queer Assemblages." *Social Text* 23, nos. 3-4 (Autumn-Winter): 121–39.

Schuster, Joshua. 1997. "Death Reckoning in the Thinking of Heidegger, Foucault, and Derrida." *Other Voices* 1, no. 1 (March): http://www.othervoices.org/1.1/jnschust/death.php (accessed 2 March 2013).

Sedgwick, Eve Kosofsky. 1994. *Tendencies.* London: Routledge.

Sholock, Adale. 2007. "Queer Theory in the First Person: Academic Autobiography and the Authoritative Contingencies of Visibility." *Cultural Critique* 66 (Spring): 127–52.

Spivak, Gayatri Chakravorty. 1977. "Glas-piece." *Diacritics* 7, no. 3: 22–45.

Wolfe Cary. 2009. *What Is Posthumanism?* Minneapolis: University of Minnesota Press.

2.1. Chapter 1: The Neuter

Barthes, Roland. 2005. *The Neutral: Lecture Course at the Collège de France (1977-1978).* Trans. R.E. Krauss and D. Hollier. New York: Columbia University Press.

Blanchot, Maurice. 1992. *The Step Not Beyond.* Trans. L. Nelson. New York: State University Press.

Chanter, Tina. 1997. "On Not Reading Derrida's Texts: Mistaking Hermeneutics, Misreading Sexual Difference, and Neutralizing Narration." In *Derrida and Feminism: Recasting the Question of Woman*, ed. Ellen K. Feder and Mary C. Rawlinson, 87–113. London: Routledge.

Cornell, Drucilla. 1997. "Where Love Begins: Sexual Difference and the Limit of the Masculine Symbolic." In *Derrida and Feminism: Recasting the Question of Woman*, ed. Ellen K. Feder and Mary C. Rawlinson, 162–206. London: Routledge.

Deleuze, Gilles. 2003. *The Logic of Sense*. Trans. M. Lester. London: Continuum.

de Saint Cheron, Michaël. 2010. *Conversations with Emmanuel Levinas, 1983-1994*. Pittsburgh: Duquesne University Press.

Heidegger, Martin. 1962. *Being and Time*. Trans. J. Macquarrie and E. Robinson. New York: Harper Collins.

—. 1972. *On Time and Being*. Trans. J. Stambaugh. New York: Harper.

—. 1984. *The Metaphysical Foundations of Logic*. Trans. M. Heim. Minneapolis: Indiana University Press.

—. 2000. *Introduction to Metaphysics*. Trans. G. Fried and R. Polt. New Haven: Yale University Press.

Kamuf, Peggy. 2001. "Derrida and Gender: the Other Sexual Difference." In *Jacques Derrida and the Humanities: A Critical Reader*, ed. Tom Cohen, 82–107. Cambridge: Cambridge University Press.

Lyotard, Jean-François. 1986. "Levinas' Logic," trans. I. McLeod, In *Face to Face with Levinas*, ed. Richard A. Cohen, 117–58. New York: State University of New York Press.

Martinon, Jean-Paul. 2013. *After 'Rwanda.'* Amsterdam: Rodopi.

Mortensen, Ellen. 2002. *Touching Thought: Ontology and Sexual Difference*. Lanham: Lexington Books.

Ouaknin, Marc-Alain. 1992. *Meditations érotiques: Essai sur Emmanuel Levinas*. Paris: Bibliotheque Payot – Editions Balland.

Voisset-Veysseyre, Cécile. 2009. "De *l'afemme*, ou la fin de l'objet homosexuel comme catégorie de sexe." In *L'Objet Homosexuel: Études, constructions, critiques*, ed. Jean-Philippe Cazier, 181–6. Mons: Sils Maria.

Wittig, Monique. 1992. *The Straight Mind and Other Essays*. Boston: Beacon Press.

2.2. Chapter 2: Sexual Difference

Brennan, Teresa, ed. 1993. *Between Feminism and Psychoanalysis*. London: Routledge.

Butler, Judith, Ernesto Laclau and Slavoj Zizek. 2000. *Contingency, Hegemony, Universality: Contemporary Dialogues on the Left*. London: Verso.

Chalier, Chaterine. 2006. *Figures du Feminin*. Paris: Des Femmes: Antoinette Fouque.

Chanter, Tina, ed. 2001a. *Feminist Interpretations of Emmanuel Levinas*. University Park: Pennsylvania State University Press.

—. 2001b. *Time, Death, and the Feminine*. Stanford: Stanford University Press.

Copjec, Joan. 2012. "The Sexual Compact." *Angelaki: Journal of the Theoretical Humanities* 17, no. 2: 31–48.

Cornell, Drucilla. 1997. "Where Love Begins: Sexual Difference and the Limit of the Masculine Symbolic." In *Derrida and Feminism: Recasting the Question of Woman*, ed. Ellen K. Feder and Mary C. Rawlinson, 162–206. London: Routledge.

Dastur, Françoise. 2000. *Telling Time, Sketch of a Phenomenological Chrono-logy*. Trans. E. Bullard. London: Athlone Press.

Gruber, Eberhard. 2006. "Autrement que sexuellement marqué? Lecture d'Emmanuel Levinas." *Literature* 142 (June): 50–69.

Halberstam, Judith. 1998. *Female Masculinity.* Durham: Duke University Press.

Heidegger, Martin. 2002. *On Being and Time.* Trans. J. Stambaugh. Chicago: University of Chicago Press.

James, Ian. 2006. *The Fragmentary Demand: An Introduction to the Philosophy of Jean-Luc Nancy.* Stanford: Stanford University Press.

Kayser, Paulette. 2000. *Emmanuel Levinas: La trace du feminin.* Paris: Presses Universitaires de France.

Irigaray, Luce. 1985a. *Speculum of the Other Woman.* Trans. G.C. Gill. Ithaca: Cornell University Press.

—. 1985b. *This Sex Which is Not One.* Trans. C. Porter and C. Burke. Ithaca: Cornell University Press.

—. 2004. "What Other Are We Talking About?" trans. E. Marion. *Yale French Studies* 104: 67–81.

Lyotard, Jean-François. 1991. *The Inhuman: Reflections on Time.* Trans. G. Bennington and R. Bowlby. Stanford: Stanford University Press.

—. 1999. *The Hyphen: between Judaism and Christianity—with Eberhard Gruber.* Trans. P.-A. Brault and M. Naas. New York: Humanities Book.

Malabou, Catherine. 2005. *La plasticité au soir de l'écriture: Dialectique, destruction, deconstruction.* Paris: Editions Léo Scheer.

—. 2011. *Changing Difference: The Feminist and the Question of Philosophy.* Trans. C. Shread. London: Polity.

Oliver, Kelly. 2009. "Sexual Difference, Animal Difference: Derrida and Difference Worthy of its Name." *Hypatia* 24, no. 2 (Spring): 290–312.

Puar, Jasbir K. 2005. "Queer Times, Queer Assemblages," *Social Text* 23, nos. 3-4 (Autumn-Winter): 121–39.

Spivak, Gayatri Chakravorty. 1984. "Love Me, Love My Ombre, Elle." *Diacritics* 14, no. 4 (Winter): 19–36.

Zuern, John. 1992. "The Future of the Phallus: Time, Mastery, and the Male Body." In *Revealing Male Bodies*, ed. Nancy Tuana, William Cowling, Maurice Hamington, Greg Johnson, and Terrance Macmullan, 55–81. Bloomington: Indiana University Press.

2.3. Chapter 3: Male

Ahmed, Sara. 2006. *Queer Phenomenology: Orientations, Objects, Others.* Durham: Duke University Press.

Aristarkhova, Irina. 2012. *Hospitality of the Matrix: Philosophy, Biomedicine, and Culture.* New York: Columbia University Press.

Berger, Maurice, Brian Wallis, and Simon Watson, eds. 1996. *Constructing Masculinity.* London: Routledge.

Bernasconi, Robert. 2005. "Levinas and the Struggle for Existence." In *Addressing Levinas*, ed. Eric Sean Nelson, Antje Kapust, and Kent Still, 170–84. Evanston: Northwestern University Press.

Brod, Harry and Michael Kaufman, eds. 1994. *Theorizing Masculinities.* London: Sage Publications.

Butler, Judith. 1990. *Gender Trouble: Feminism and the Subversion of Identity.* London: Routledge.

—. 2005. *Giving an Account of Oneself.* New York: Fordham University Press.

Chalier, Catherine. 1991. "Ethics and the Feminine." In *Re-Reading Levinas*, ed. Robert Bernasconi and Simon Critchley, 11–47. London: Athlone Press.

—. 2001. "The Exteriority of the Feminine," trans. B. Bergo. In *Feminist Interpretations of Emmanuel Levinas*, ed. Tina Chanter, 171–9. University Park: Penn State University Press.

Cohen, Richard A, ed. 1986. *Face to Face with Levinas*. Albany: State University of New York Press.

—. 1994. *Elevations: The Height of the Good in Rosenzweig and Levinas*. Chicago: University of Chicago Press.

Corbett, Ken. 2009. *Boyhoods: Rethinking Masculinities*. New Haven: Yale University Press.

Grosz, Elizabeth. 1995. *Space, Time, and Perversion: Essays on the Politics of Bodies*. London: Routledge.

Hoquet, Thierry. 2009. *La Virility: A quoi rêvent les hommes*. Paris: Larousse.

Jagose, Annamarie. 2002. *Inconsequence: Lesbian Representation and the Logic of Sexual Sequence*. New York: Cornell University Press.

Taylor, Chloé. 2006. "Hard, Dry Eyes and Eyes That Weep: Vision and Ethics in Levinas and Derrida." *Postmodern Culture* 16, no. 2 (January).

Thomas, Calvin. 1996. *Male Matters: Masculinities, Anxiety, and the Male Body on the Line*. Chicago: University of Illinois Press.

2.4. Chapter 4: Side Story

Aydemir, Murat. 2007. *Images of Bliss: Ejaculation, Masculinity, Meaning*. Minneapolis: University of Minnesota Press.

Bal, Mieke. 1985. "Sexuality, Sin and Sorrow: The Emergence of the Female Character (A Reading of Genesis 1-3)." *Poetics Today* 6, no. 1/2: 21–42.

Bloom, Harold. 1984. "Criticism, Canon-Formation, and Prophecy: The Sorrows of Facticity." *Raritan* 3, no. 3: 1–20.

Bowie, Malcom. 2000. *Proust Among the Stars*. New York: Columbia University Press.

Boyarin, Daniel. 1990. "The Politics of Biblical Narratology: Reading the Bible Like/As a Woman." *Diacritics* 20: 31–42.

—. 1995. *Carnal Israel: Reading Sex in Talmudic Culture.* Berkeley: University of California Press.

Cohn-Eskenazi, Tamara, Gary A. Phillips and David Jobling, eds. 2003. *Levinas and Biblical Studies.* New York: Society of Biblical Literature.

Critchley, Simon. 1999. *The Ethics of Deconstruction: Derrida and Levinas.* Edinburgh: Edinburgh University Press.

de Beauvoir, Simone. 1952. *The Second Sex.* Trans. H.M. Parshley. New York: Alfred A. Knopf.

Duncan, Diane Moira. 2001. *The Pre-Text of Ethics: On Derrida and Levinas.* Bern: Peter Lang.

Froula, Christine. 1988. "Rewriting Genesis: Gender and Culture in Twentieth-Century Texts." *Tulsa Studies in Women's Literature* 7, no. 2 (Autumn): 197–220.

Heidegger, Martin. 2008. *Ontology—The Hermeneutics of Facticity* [1988]. Trans. J. van Buren. Bloomington: Indiana University Press.

Irigaray, Luce. 2013. *In the Beginning, She Was.* London: Bloomsbury.

Katz, Claire Elise. 2003. *Levinas, Judaism and the Feminine: The Silent Footsteps of Rebecca.* Bloomington: Indiana University Press.

Laruelle, François, ed. 1997. *Textes pour Emmanuel Levinas.* Paris: J.-M. Place.

Meillassoux, Quentin. 2008. *After Finitude: An Essay on the Necessity of Contingency.* Trans. R. Brassier. London: Continuum.

Ouaknin, Marc-Alain. 1992. *Meditations érotiques: Essai sur Emmanuel Levinas.* Paris: Bibliotheque Payot – Editions Balland.

Plato. 1951. *Symposium* [416 BCE]. Trans. W. Hamilton. London: Penguin.

Proust, Marcel. 2003. *In Search of Lost Time: The Way by Swann's.* Vol. 1. Trans. L. Davis. London: Penguin Classics.

Reik, Thomas. 1960. *The Creation of Woman: A Psychoanalytic Inquiry into the Myth of Eve*. New York: George Braziller.

Reisenberger, Azila Talit. 1993. "The Creation of Adam as Hermaphrodite and its Implications for Feminist Theology." *Judaism: A Quarterly Journal of Jewish Life and Thought* (Autumn): 1–4.

Trible, Phyllis. 1978. *God and the Rhetoric of Sexuality*. Philadelphia: Fortress.

—. 1984. *Texts of Terror: Literary-Feminist Readings of Biblical Narratives*. Philadelphia: Fortress.

2.5. Chapter 5: End(s) Meet

Barthes, Roland. 2002. *A Lover's Discourse: Fragments*. Trans. R. Howard. London: Vintage.

Bersani, Leo. 1987. "Is the Rectum a Grave?" *October* 43 (Winter): 197–222.

Butler, Judith. 2005. "On Never Having Learned How to Live." *Differences* 16, no. 3: 27–34.

—. 2010. *Bodies That Matter: On The Discursive Limits of 'Sex'* [1993]. London: Routledge.

Cazier, Jean-Philippe. 2009. "L'Objet homosexuel – De l'objet ou sujet?" In *L'Objet Homosexuel: Études, constructions, critiques*, ed. Jean-Philippe Cazier, 7–16. Mons: Éditions Sils Maria.

Chanter, Tina. 1994. *Ethics of Eros: Irigaray's Re-writing of the Philosophers*. London: Routledge.

Cixous, Hélène. 2006. "Nous en somme." *Littérature* 2, no. 142: 102–12.

Dean, Tim. 2009. *Unlimited Intimacy: Reflections on the Subculture of Barebacking*. Chicago: University of Chicago Press.

Deleuze, Gilles. 1995. *Negotiations, 1972-1990*. Trans. M. Joughin. New York: Columbia University Press.

Derrida, Jacques. 2004. "Je suis en guerre contre moi-même." *Le Monde* (18 Aug. 2004).

Edelman, Lee. 1994. *Homographesis: Essays in Gay Literary and Cultural Theory*. London: Routledge.

—. 2005. *No Future: Queer Theory and the Death Drive*. Durham: Duke University Press.

Eribon, Didier. 2004. *Insult and the Making of the Gay Self* [1999]. Trans. M. Lucey. Durham: Duke University Press.

Foucault, Michel. 1990. *Care of the Self: The History of Sexuality*. Vol 3. Trans. R. Hurley. London: Penguin.

—. 1992. *The Use of Pleasure: The History of Sexuality*. Vol 2. Trans. R. Hurley. London: Penguin Books.

—. 1998. *The History of Sexuality: The Will to Knowledge: The History of Sexuality*. Vol. 1. Trans. R. Hurley. London: Penguin Books.

Freccero, Carla. 2005. *Queer/Early/Modern*. Durham: Duke University Press.

—. 2006. "Fuck the Future." *GLQ: A Journal of Lesbian and Gay Studies* 12, no. 2: 332–34.

Freud, Sigmund. 1922. *On Sexuality: Three Essays on the Theory of Sexuality*. Trans. J. Stachey. Harmondsworth: Penguin Books.

Fuss, Diana. 1991. *Inside/Out: Lesbian Theories, Gay Theories*. London: Routledge.

Greenberg, Steven. 2004. *Wrestling with God and Men: Homosexuality in the Jewish Tradition*. Madison: University of Winsconsin Press.

Hocquenghem Guy. 1993. *Homosexual Desire* [1972]. Trans. D. Dangoor. Durham: Duke University Press.

—. 2010. *The Screwball Asses* [1973]. Trans. N. Wedell. Cambridge: Semiotext(e).

Ince, K.L. 1996. "Questions to Luce Irigaray." *Hypatia* 11, no. 1: 122–40.

Irigaray, Luce. 2001. "The Fecundity of the Caress: A Reading of Levinas' *Totality and Infinity* and 'Phenomenology of Eros'," trans. B. Burke and G. Gill. In *Feminist Interpretations of Emmanuel Levinas*, ed. Tina Chanter, 119–44. Pennsylvania: Pennsylvania University Press.

Muñoz, José Esteban. 2009. *Cruising Utopia: The Then and There of Queer Futurity.* New York: New York University Press.

Oliver, Kelly. 1997. "Fatherhood and the Promise of Ethics." *Diacritics* 27, no. 1 (Spring): 45–57.

—. 2001. "Paternal Election and the Absent Father." In *Feminist Interpretations of Emmanuel Levinas*, ed. Tina Chanter, 224–40. Pennsylvania: Pennsylvania University Press.

Sedgwick, Eve Kosofsky. 1991. *Epistemology of the Closet.* Berkeley: University of California Press.

Ziarek, Ewa Plonowska. 2001. "The Ethical Passions of Emmanuel Levinas." In *Feminist Interpretations of Emmanuel Levinas*, ed. Tina Chanter, 78–95. Pennsylvania: Pennsylvania University Press.

2.6. Chapter 6: The Factory

Apollinaire, Guillaume. 2004. *The Debauched Hospodar.* Trans. O. Mole. London: Olympia Press.

Aquinas, Thomas. 1967. *Summa theologiae.* Trans. T. Gilby. London: Blackfriars.

Bataille, Georges. 1991. *The Accursed Share.* Vol. 1. Trans. R. Hurley. Cambridge: MIT Press.

Brodribb, Somer. 1992. "Reproductive and Genetic Engineering." *Journal of International Feminist Analysis* 5, no. 3: 24–57.

de Verville, François Béroalde. 2003. *Le Moyen de parvenir.* St Brieuc: Passage du Nord-Ouest.

Diderot, Denis. 1957. "Lettre à Damilaville, 3 novembre 1760." In *Correspondance*, Vol. III (novembre 1759 - décembre 1761), ed. Georges Roth. Paris: Minuit.

Douglas, Mary. 2002. *Purity and Danger: An Analysis of Concepts of Pollution and Taboo.* London: Routledge.

Esposito, Roberto. 2009. *Communitas: The Origin and Destiny of Community.* Trans. T.C. Campbell. Stanford: Stanford University Press.

Gaudillière, Jean-Paul. 2004. "On ne naît pas homme... À propos de la construction biologique du masculine." *Mouvements* 1, no. 31: 15–23; doi: 10.3917/mouv.031.0015.

Halberstam, Judith. 2002. "The Good, the Bad, and the Ugly: Men, Women, and Masculinity." In *Masculinity Studies and Feminist Theory: New Directions,* ed. Judith Kegan Gardiner, 344–67. New York: Columbia University Press.

Herbold, Sarah. 1995. "Well-Placed Reflections: (Post)modern Woman as Symptom of (Post)modern Man." *Signs* 21, no. 1 (Autumn): 83–115.

Katz, Joshua T. 1998. "Testimonia Ritus Italici: Male Genitalia, Solemn Declarations, and a New Latin Sound Law." *Harvard Studies in Classical Philology* 98: 183–217.

Kristeva, Julia. 1982. *Powers of Horror: An Essay on Abjection.* Trans. L.S. Roudiez. New York: Columbia University Press.

McManus, I. C. 1976. "Scrotal Asymmetry in Man and in Ancient Sculpture." *Nature* 4: 359–426.

Montrelay, Michèle. 1982. "L'Appareillage." *Cahiers Confrontations* 6 (Spring): 33–43.

O'Brien, Mary. 1989. *The Politics of Reproduction.* London: Routledge & Paul Kegan.

Oliver, Kelly. 2001. "Paternal Election and the Absent Father." In *Feminist interpretations of Emmanuel Levinas,* ed. Tina Chanter, 224–41. University Park: Pennsylvania State University Press.

Plautus. 2011. *Curculio.* Trans. W. De Melo. London: Loeb.

Reich, Wilhelm. 1986. *The Function of the Orgasm: Sex-Economic Problems of Biological Energy.* Trans. V.R. Carfagno. New York: Farrar, Straus and Giroux.

Rousseau, Jean-Jacques. 2000. *Confessions.* Trans. A. Scholar. Oxford: Oxford Paperbacks.

Schneider, Monique. 2011. "Le corps masculin: une production culturelle?" *Champ psychosomatique* 1, no. 59: 15–29; doi: 10.3917/cpsy.059.0015.

Smith, Paul. 1988. "Vas." *Camera Obscura* 6, no. 2 (May): 89–111.

Taylor, Gary. 2002. *An Abbreviated History of Castration of Western Manhood.* London: Routledge.

Vié, Blandine. 2001. *Testicles.* Trans. G. MacDonogh. Totnes: Prospect Books.

Zizek, Slavoj. 1989. *The Sublime Object of Ideology.* London: Verso.

2.7. Chapter 7: Couplings

Bankovsky, Miriam. 2004. "A Thread of Knots: Jacques Derrida's Homage to Emmanuel Levinas's Ethical Reminder." *Invisible Culture* 8: http://hdl.handle.net/1802/3559 (accessed 19 October 2012).

Blanchot, Maurice. 1993. *The Infinite Conversation.* Trans. S. Hanson. Minneapolis: University of Minnesota Press.

Caputo, John D. 1997. "Dreaming of the Innumerable: Derrida, Drucilla Cornell, and the Dance of Gender." In *Derrida and Feminism: Recasting the Question of Woman,* ed. Ellen K. Feder and Mary C. Rawlinson, 141–60. London: Routledge.

Cassuto, Umberto. 1961. *A Commentary on the Book of Genesis.* Trans. I. Abrahams. Jerusalem: Magnes Press.

Colebrook, Claire. 1997. "Feminist Philosophy and Philosophy of Feminism: Luce Irigaray and the History of Western Metaphysics." *Hypatia* 12, no. 1 (Winter): 79–98.

Cornell, Drucilla. 1997. "Where Love Begins: Sexual Difference and the Limit of the Masculine Symbolic." In *Derrida and Feminism: Recasting the Question of Woman*, ed. Ellen K. Feder and Mary C. Rawlinson, 162–206. London: Routledge.

Grosz, Elizabeth. 2012. "The Nature of Sexual Difference." *Angelaki: Journal of the Theoretical Humanities* 17, no. 2: 69–93.

Kayser, Paulette. 2000. *Emmanuel Levinas: La trace du feminin*. Paris: Presses Universitaires de France.

Keller, Catherine. 2007. "Rumours of Transcendence: The Movement, State, and Sex of Beyond." In *Transcendence and Beyond: A Postmodern Inquiry*, ed. John D. Caputo and Michael J. Scanlon, 129–50. Minneapolis: Indiana University Press.

Kristeva, Julia. 1981. "Women's Time." *Signs* 7, no. 1 (Autumn): 13–35.

Lingis, Alphonso. 1985. "Phenomenology of the Face and Carnal Intimacy." In *Libido: The French Existential Theories*, 58–73. Bloomington: Indiana University Press.

Manning, Robert. 1991. "Thinking the Other Without Violence? An Analysis of the Relations Between the Philosophy of Emmanuel Levinas and Feminism." *The Journal of Speculative Philosophy* 5, no. 2: 132–43.

Priest, Ann-Marie. 2003. "Woman as God, God as Woman: Mysticism, Negative Theology, and Luce Irigaray." *The Journal of Religion* 83, no. 1 (January): 1–17.

Reisenberger, Azila Talit. 1993. "The Creation of Adam as Hermaphrodite and its Implications for Feminist Theology." *Judaism: A Quarterly Journal of Jewish Life and Thought* 43 (September): 1–6.

Rivière, Joan. 1929. "Womanliness as a masquerade." *International Journal of Psychoanalysis* 10: 303–13.

Rawlinson, Mary C. 1997. "Levers, Signatures, and Secrets: Derrida's Use of Woman." In *Derrida and Feminism: Recasting the Question of Woman,* ed. Ellen K. Feder and Mary C. Rawlinson, 69–85. London: Routledge.

Schües, Christina, Dorothea E. Olkowski and Helen A. Fielding eds. 2011. *Time in Feminist Phenomenology.* Bloomington: Indiana University Press.

Shapiro, Susan E. 2000. "On Thinking Identity Otherwise." In *Mapping Jewish Identities: New Perspectives on Jewish Studies,* ed. Laurence Silberstein, 299–323. New York: New York University Press.